REFERENCE AND COLLECTION DEVELOPMENT ON THE INTERNET

A How-To-Do-It Manual

Elizabeth Thomsen

**HOW-TO-DO-IT MANUALS
FOR LIBRARIANS**

NUMBER 66

NEAL-SCHUMAN PUBLISHERS, INC.
New York, London

Published by Neal-Schuman Publishers, Inc.
100 Varick Street
New York, NY 10013

Printed and bound in the United States of America.

Library of Congress Cataloging-in-Publication Data

Thomsen, Elizabeth
    Reference and collection development on the Internet / Elizabeth
Thomsen.
        p.   cm. — (How-to-do-it manuals ; no. 66)
    Includes bibliographical references and index.
    ISBN 1-55570-243-0 (alk. paper)
    1. Reference services (Libraries—United States).   2. Collection
development (Libraries)—United States .   3. Internet (Computer
network).   I. Title.   II. Series: How-do-do-it
    Z711.T487   1996
    025.04—dc20   96-14737

CONTENTS

FIGURES

FOREWORD

The other day I was sitting in my car waiting to pick up a veggie burrito in a fast food drive-thru lane. The tailgate of the pickup truck in front me was emblazoned with, "See our web page at http://www.autoglass.com" (or some such address). As I looked at this, my radio blared an advertisement for an upcoming Internet training seminar sponsored by a local newspaper, only to be followed by another ad encouraging subscriptions to a national Internet magazine. It was a striking moment for me, which demonstrated the pervasiveness of the Net. The future is clearly now for Cyberspace.

With the hyping and seeming omnipresence of the Internet, an excellent tool for librarians can be lost by the public in the "cyberroar." We librarians are THE information specialists—we know a good resource when we see one. More than any other, we can look at the Internet with a cool eye toward practicality, and away from the clamor. For us, the Internet is merely another arrow for our information quiver.

Getting to the point of using the Internet consistently is difficult, though. It is a vast resource, one that gets bigger and more complicated with each passing day. Librarians are busy enough, and we need all the help we can get.

Enter Elizabeth Thomsen. In *Reference and Collection Development on the Internet: A How-To-Do-It Manual for Librarians*, Elizabeth provides an excellent, practical guide for using the Internet in the real world. An accomplished Internet surfer and librarian, Elizabeth combines these skills to make sense of the bewildering Net landscape. She focuses on the Internet as a communications tool, and as a dynamic resource to develop library collections. These are the areas where the Internet is important for our professional development and work. Elizabeth demonstrates how to do this; how to use the Internet to learn from others.

Whether you're a long time Internet user, or a novice, your time will not be wasted reading this book. With netmania raging everywhere, it's great to have a text that calmly provides librarians practical information.

John Iliff on Coquina Key in Florida
Head Reference and Systems Administrator
http://snoopy.tblc.lib.fl.us/pppl/pppl.html
Pinellas Park Public Library 7770 52 Street, Pinellas Park, FL 34665
(813) 541-0719 (Fax) 541-0818
E-mail: PP001654@interramp.com and co-moderator of the publib listserv.

PREFACE

The Internet is everywhere these days: in our homes and schools, on the front pages of newspapers and on magazine covers. The rapid growth of the Internet is one of the most amazing phenomena of our times. It is changing our lives and our society at the end of the twentieth century as much as the introduction of the automobile did at the beginning, so it is perhaps not surprising that the Information Superhighway label has caught on. We speak of onramps and roadmaps, and as more and more people start cruising, of traffic jams and roadkill.

Although we call this the Information Superhighway, the Internet is not really a source of information, but rather a means of communication. The Internet fosters two types of communication. One is conversation, often carried on through e-mail groups and USENET newsgroups. These groups generally form around a shared area of interest, which can be professional, scholarly, recreational, or social. These interest groups are not unlike similar groups which have real meetings, and they provide a way for people to share ideas and information about a particular subject. The Internet, however, allows these groups to transcend the barriers of time and space that limit participation in other types of organizations.

The other type of communication is online publishing. The Internet provides a way for any person or organization to publish information and make it easily available, usually through a World Wide Web site. The Web has made it possible for almost anyone to set up his or her own information service. The Internet has become a populist information utility, allowing anyone with sufficient interest and skill to become an independent information agent.

As others enthusiastically jump on the Internet bandwagon, librarians face some special challenges. The first is that our professional training and temperament gives us a distinct preference for organized, stable information resources from identifiable, authoritative sources. The inherently chaotic and volatile nature of the Internet is both a professional anathema and an opportunity for us to exhibit our ability to organize and retrieve information. Both the opportunity and the challenge presented by the Internet are particularly applicable to us as reference and collection development librarians.

Reference librarians constantly seek information for other people. If I am a home user of the Internet, I might have three or four areas of interest, for example, the Civil War, roller coasters, UNIX, and dog breeding. I find groups devoted to these interests, and through these groups find out about all sorts of relevant Internet resources. Within a few weeks, I feel comfortable in these areas and find that the Internet is a wonderful source of information. The average reference librarian, however, doesn't have the luxury of exploring a few subject areas in depth, but is constantly jumping from subject to subject on behalf of patrons. This makes it much harder for us to develop a sense of familiarity. You may find a great Civil War site when working with one patron, and then not be asked another Civil War question for a year.

Collection development librarians often feel even less comfortable exploring the Internet. The best known aspects of the Internet are government information (Supreme Court rulings, text of pending legislation, etc.), popular culture resources and other random, personal projects. None of these has immediate appeal for collection development librarians, who are looking for authoritative, professional, and evaluative sources. In addition, collection Development Librarians may resent the frequent references that the Internet is making books obsolete. However, collection development librarians, however, who explore e-mail groups and USENET newsgroups will find that books are frequently and lovingly discussed, and that lists of recommended books are becoming a standard component of subject-oriented World Wide Web sites.

Like their colleagues in other areas of the profession, many reference and collection development librarians share an important handicap. Many librarians, especially in public libraries, have more limited access to the Internet than the average home user or college student. Many libraries have access via terminals and telecommunications networks that were designed for circulation and online catalog systems. This often limits us to Lynx, a text-based World Wide Web browser, rather that the graphical browsers that are becoming standard. This is a serious handicap, and makes it difficult for us to relate to the World Wide Web that we see in magazines and on television. Librarians are also far less apt to have access to USENET news than college students and home users. And, finally, librarians often share accounts or workstations, which makes it harder to set preferences and maintain bookmarks. Despite these handicaps, librarians have much to gain and much to contribute from active participation in the Internet. We can find the answers to frequently asked questions, seek recommendations for books to add to our collections, and help guide our patrons as they explore this exciting but often confusing new world.

The purpose of this book is to give reference and collection development librarians a sense of the Internet as a community of individuals and organizations who share information through online conversations and online resources. The focus is on resources that are new and evolving and reflect the populist nature of the Internet. These resources are an invaluable way for librarians to tap into the interests, questions, and recommendations of people who reflect the needs of our own patrons.

This first part of the book, Chapters 1 and 2, includes a history of the Internet with a special emphasis on the Internet as a community, and an overview of the tools of the trade—Internet basics that everyone should know as they venture out into the Internet.

The second part, Chapters 3–8, discusses how reference and collection development librarians can use Internet fundamentals (e-mail, USENET newsgroups, Gopher, and the World Wide Web) and special resources (library catalogs, databases, electronic books, and Frequently Asked Questions files) to better serve their patrons. A special chapter in this part of the book, Chapter 5, is devoted to one newsgroups, rec.arts.books, which is perhaps the single best source of reference and information on the Net for reference and collection development purposes.

The third and final part of the book is comprised of two appendices. The first, The Virtual Vertical File, is a very selective compilation of Web sources which can serve as a starting point for a reference tour of the Internet. Included sites were selected on the basis of content, organization, and presentation of information frequently needed in reference works. The other appendix, the List of Lists, is a subject arrangement of booklists on the Internet that will be useful for all librarians involved in collection development and readers' advisory work. Also selective, included are sites range from bestseller lists to mythology booklists.

The Internet is changing our lives and our work as librarians, and yet, the more things change, the more they remain the same. We still need to find information for our patrons, and help them find information for themselves. We still need to build and organize collections of resources for our patrons, whether the collections are print, media, online, or a complex combination. We still need to observe Ranganathan's Law, "Save the Time of the Reader," whether the reader is reading a book or a computer screen.

There's a whole new world of information out there on the Internet that can help you serve your community. *Reference and Collection Development* is designed to help you serve your community better and more efficiently by teaching you to use the latest technology to your advantage.

1 THE LIBRARIAN AS PART OF THE INTERNET COMMUNITY

The Internet is a strange and complicated world, with its own history, traditions and culture. It is a rapidly evolving community, sometimes compared to the Wild West. In this analogy, we would now be at the turning point, where the schoolmarms have arrived, various institutions have been established, and things are just beginning to settle down. Librarians cannot afford to be left out of this evolving world.

Like libraries, the Internet is all about providing information and stimulating communication. Reference service is the business of providing people with information that they want and need. Collection development is the business of providing our users with the kind of materials that they want and need. These two aspects of librarianship are inextricably linked. Reference provides immediate answers to specific questions, and collection development provides additional resources for our users to explore their own interests. Reference and collection development are traditional library services; yet they are inevitably transformed by the Internet. By learning about this new world and participating in it, we can enhance these traditional services, as well as offer new ones.

THE HISTORY OF THE INTERNET

Over the last few years, the Internet's history has become a familiar story. The origin of the Internet goes back to the Cold War, and the birth of ARPAnet, the network of the Advanced Research Projects Agency of the Department of Defense. ARPAnet was based on packet switching technology, which would allow data to be transmitted in electronic envelopes or packets, from one computer to another following the quickest route.

An analogy for packet switching is passing notes in school. If I am sitting in the left front corner of the classroom, and I want to pass a note to my friend in the right back corner of the room, I don't need to plot the whole route from my seat to my friend's. I just write her name on the note, and pass it to the person behind me. That person sees which direction the note needs to go, and sends it off in the right general direction. The note travels from hand to hand until it reaches my friend. Each person who handles the note behaves as a router, deciding which way to pass it, based on who is sitting in his seat and who is willing to aid in the process. On three different days, the note could travel three different routes and still wind up in the right place.

This is how traffic travels on the Internet as well. The Internet is composed of a complex web of phone lines, owned by various organizations, with many different paths between any two points, and no central switching station. Each point along the Internet utilizes electronic routers programmed to know about nearby routers; Internet traffic, such as e-mail, passes from router to router, finding the best path.

The original ARPAnet was planned this way so that communications could continue even if an enemy destroyed certain sites. Today, this basic system of routing allows Internet traffic to find its way around down systems, line problems, and through traffic jams. This, and the fact that the Internet is now global, is also why censorship on the Internet is generally ineffective. The Internet sees censorship as damage, and simply routes around it.

ARPAnet began operations in 1970, and in only two years had grown to forty sites. It allows a user at one site to log-in and have terminal access at another site, to transfer files from one system to another, and to send messages from one user to another. These early activities became telnet, FTP (File Transfer Protocol) and e-mail, the three building blocks of all Internet activity.

Eventually, in the 1980s, the ARPAnet, which had been renamed the DARPAnet, turned into the NSFNet, the National Science Foundation Network. NSFNet connected government, military, and university sites primarily to support government-sponsored research. NSFNet's high speed links connecting regional computer networks have been compared to the Interstate Highway system, which provides high speed connections between the state highways which in turn connect local streets.

By the late 1980s, the true Internet had emerged from this system of interconnected regional networks. The Internet now is a network of networks, with commercial systems currently as much a part of the system as the government, military, and educational institutions that originally were linked parts of the earlier systems. The Internet is also global, not national, in scope, linking systems and networks around the world.

BEYOND THE INTERNET

Tracing the traditional history from ARPAnet to NSFNet to Internet is like tracing the traditional history of the United States from the English colonies, neglecting the early history of places like Alaska, Texas, California, and Hawaii, and considering them in relation to the developing country which annexed them. In the 1970s and 1980s, there were other developing networks that had nothing to do with the ARPAnet or NSFNet, and yet were a major influence on a generation of computer users and their experiences and expectations of life online.

ONLINE SERVICES

Commercial online services, such as Prodigy, America Online, and CompuServe were developed to provide access to online services, including online encyclopedias and other information services, online versions of magazines, and shopping services. Users pay a fee for such services, which operate on a publishing or broadcast model. The service buys the rights to professionally-produced information services, provides an interface, and then sells access to users for a fee, sometimes also selling advertising rights on the service.

The giant online services, CompuServe, Prodigy, and America Online also developed discussion forums on a variety of subjects. Because these are organizations with membership agreements and a staff to enforce order, the discussion forums on these online services are subject to more control than you would find generally on the Internet. Some people view this as a benefit while others see it as censorship.

As the Internet has grown, so have the online services, and the distinction between these services and the Internet has begun to blur. The services have long offered e-mail between their own users, but have gradually added gateways to allow their members to exchange e-mail with Internet addresses. More recently, the services have begun offering access to the World Wide Web.

BULLETIN BOARD SYSTEMS

On the other end of the spectrum, there are thousands of small, local Bulletin Board Systems, or BBSs. Many BBSs are devoted to a particular subject or theme, while others are general. Some are free and others charge fees for membership or use. BBSs tend to have a counterculture flavor to them, and they often have names like "Scream of the Butterfly" and "The Forbidden Zone."

BBSs began in the late 1970s, and at first were used to support the interests of computer hobbyists. The early BBSs provided a way to exchange software and tips about using the various types of new personal computers. By the 1980s, Bulletin Board Systems devoted to a wide variety of political, social, religious, and general interests were found all across the country.

To start a BBS, a person just needs a low-end computer, a modem, a phone line, and some inexpensive BBS software. Because a BBS is the property of one person, generally operating out of his or her own home, a BBS can be as tightly regulated or loosely controlled as the owner, generally called the *sysop* or System Operator, sees fit.

Many BBSs have local discussion groups, and many BBSs also participate in cooperative arrangements to exchange discussion groups with other BBS systems. For example, many BBSs use Fido software, and are loosely organized into FidoNet, a network that allows the passing of messages from one BBS to another. Every night, FidoNet BBSs dial up other nearby systems to exchange messages for a variety of topics, including pet care, diets, sailing, and various political topics. The FidoNet groups are called *echoes* and a FidoNet BBS may carry hundreds of different echoes or only a few on various subjects. In addition to FidoNet, there are a number of other BBS networks, including Smartnet, RelayNet, KinkNet, and Ilink.

The BBS world developed on a different model than either the early Internet—which was controlled by government and university systems—or the commercial online systems—which were and are controlled by businesses. Dialing up a local BBS was the first experience of online culture for thousands of people, and the low cost of starting and running a BBS gave many people a chance to be service providers and rulers of their own small online kingdoms.

BBSs are still around, but most have now developed connections and ties to USENET and the Internet. Many local Internet Service Providers are sysops who are adding a new dimension to their BBSs.

AS THE ELECTRONIC WATERING HOLE

We speak of the Information Superhighway and use a host of bold and exciting ocean-based metaphors related to navigation and surfing, but the best metaphor for the Internet as most of us experience it is perhaps not the sea of information but the watering hole, or even the water cooler. There are many sources of information on the Internet, including searchable databases and hypertext information systems, but while these are all useful sources, they are impersonal. Most people don't want to read information about their interests or download encyclopedic articles and databases nearly as much as they want to have electronic conversations with other people who share their interests.

While the Internet is often promoted as a source of information, its primary benefit for most people is communication. Human beings have a deep need to form groups, and the Internet and other online systems have given us a whole new way to form associations and communities of interest.

TRANSCENDING TIME AND SPACE

There are some special aspects of communicating via computer that are worth examination. The first is the ability to use networks to transcend the ordinary barriers of time and space.

We transcend time when we use e-mail groups or USENET newsgroups, which are *asynchronous* in nature. The telephone, in contrast is an inherently *synchronous* means of communication. To talk to me on the telephone, you and I have to synchronize our lives during our conversation. The patron who calls you on the phone to ask a reference question has no way of knowing whether or not this is a good time or how many other patrons are lined up at the Reference Desk waiting to ask their questions. The telephone rings, and we respond in real time, synchronizing ourselves with another. In asynchronous communication, someone leaves a message at his convenience, and another person responds in her own time. Telephone answering machines and voice mail, memos, and notes are other examples of asynchronous communication.

Synchronous communication is particularly suited to two situations: intimacy and urgency. In intimate situations, we may cherish the feeling that we are temporarily synchronized or connected with another. In urgent situations, where time is of the essence, we may need immediate attention.

Asynchronous communication, however, has many of its own advantages. Because each party contributes when he chooses, communication is often more open and relaxed. Nobody is being interrupted in asynchronous communication. E-mail and USENET can make it possible for people with very busy lives to find the time to engage in discussions at their own convenience.

Transcending space is another benefit. Many people find themselves feeling lonely and isolated much of the time. This may be because they live in a remote rural area, or because they live in an area where they feel unsafe going out after dark. Other people are isolated due to family responsibilities, such as caring for young children or chronically ill family members.

These new forums transcend geographical boundaries as well. In all the groups, people share casual conversation with others from many different countries. Although the conversation centers on a specific subject, such as cooking, movies, or Medieval art, the presence of people from all over the world brings new perspectives to all the participants.

AN INCLUSIVE SOCIETY

There are other benefits to the inclusiveness of these groups. On the groups, you are not judged on the basis of your age, gender, race, or appearance, but on the basis of your words. This is an aspect of the Internet that can be abused, and everyone has heard stories of people who misrepresent themselves. It's not uncommon on the social groups for people to impersonate members of the other gender. There is even an infamous impostor who has a convincing e-mail address and signature file identifying him as a nun who then shocks newcomers with some surprising messages. But beyond the abuse, there is a great deal of honest, genuine, helpful conversation among people who know each other only by their words.

This type of communication provides a unique opportunity for physically handicapped people as well, who can escape the isolation that their conditions may impose and be able to communicate easily with others. Hearing impaired people find computer-mediated communication to be as freeing to them as the telephone has been restricting. Visually handicapped people can use systems which read the screen, which in turn frees them to communicate via e-mail without the problems of regular print. In fact, there is adaptive technology that allows almost anyone to use a computer, and over and over the word *freeing* is used by visually or hearing impaired people who have discovered the joy of e-mail.

The great advantage for many such users is the ability to handle their own communication, without the need for another person to act as mediator. Norman Coombs has written an eloquent essay called "Your Onramp to the Internet: The Power of Electronic Mail," in which he describes some of his experiences using e-mail in the academic environment. Professor Coombs teaches at the Rochester Institute of Technology, and shares some of his experiences:

The Rochester Institute of Technology has the National Technical Institute for the Deaf on its campus and is home to several hundred hearing impaired students. When I began having my class submit their papers on e-mail, one of the first papers was from a deaf girl. This led to our exchanging two or three messages about the paper and the grade. Then, she sent e-mail telling me that this was the first time in her life she had been able to talk with a professor without having someone, an interpreter, in the middle. The irony is, that because I am blind, we had to transcend a double communication barrier.[1]

Elizabeth Eisenhood, a deaf librarian who works at the Washington Talking Book Library, writes,

We serve people with a range of disabilities, including speech impairment and deaf-blindness . . . I have a small but faithful group of patrons who give me their reference questions via Internet. It has eased the accessibility issues on both sides of the desk, since, if they are using a computer, I know that they have whatever output devices they need on their end, and I don't have to deal with phone issues on mine.[2]

Both Norman Coombs and Elizabeth Eisenhood use e-mail regularly both for individual communication with students and patrons, and for participating in discussion groups and expanding their professional interests. Professor Coombs writes that, "The ability to share in discussion lists without needing a reader or other assistant is a freeing and exhilarating experience,"[3] and Elizabeth Eisenhood enthusiastically agrees, noting that "Internet e-mail has given me a worldwide group of colleagues . . . without concerns of communication."[4]

Professor Coombs' interest in new possibilities for communication extend beyond visual and hearing impairments, and he writes, "While we normally do not classify shyness as a disability, many inhibited people interact more readily and more openly using computer mediated communication than they will in person."[5]

In fact, the uninhibited nature of online communication also causes problems. Sitting at home alone at the computer, often late at night, people sometimes open up a little more than they really should. Sometimes there are vitriolic exchanges on controversial issues, and sometimes there are personal attacks that quickly degenerate into arguments of the "Oh, yeah?" "Yeah!" "Who says?" "I say" variety.

A more subtle problem can arise when people use a forum as a support group, confessional, or soapbox. Even in the professional groups, people will sometimes talk about their supervisors, colleagues, trustees, and patrons in a way they never would in a public place, not realizing that the Internet is a very public place.

Most groups have far more readers than participants, and it's a mistake to forget that your messages can be read by people who know you. Messages can be forwarded around, and often live forever in searchable archives. Don't say anything in the online forums that you wouldn't say at a public meeting in your own town.

ETIQUETTE ONLINE

There is an online culture with its own language, legends, and etiquette. A basic understanding of the nature of online communication and common sense are the best guides to bridging this culture.

Sometimes the arguments that crop up in various groups are attributed to misunderstandings caused by the lack of visual cues, such as expression, and auditory cues, such as tone of voice, that would be necessary to properly understanding a message. To compensate, some people use punctuation signs to indicate mood, like this: :-) a smiley face, to indicate happiness, a frown like this: :-(to indicate unhappiness. The faces have many variations, and are sometimes called *emoticons*.

Electronic communication, however, uses the written word, and people have used the written word to communicate complex ideas and emotions for hundreds of years without needing the little symbols of expression. It's difficult to imagine Dickens writing

It was the best of times :-)
It was the worst of times :-(

In addition to the faces, many abbreviations are used on the Internet. For example, IMHO is short for In My Humble Opinion, TIA means Thanks in Advance, and HTH means Hope This Helps.

In general, it's a good idea to read messages in a new group for a few weeks to observe the style and type of postings that are standard. Some groups are very informal and are full of running jokes and emoticons. Professional groups tend to be much more formal.

Most rules for online communication are the same as the rules for any other civilized discourse. For example, personal attacks are never appropriate. Chain letters and "get rich quick" schemes are junk mail whatever the means of delivery. Advertising is restricted to certain groups, and is an unwelcome intrusion elsewhere. It is rude to expect other people to do your homework for you. (Questions with the phrase "compare and contrast" in them are a dead giveaway.) It is also rude to ask a question on a group read by thousands of people if the question could easily be answered with a slight amount of personal effort, for example, asking for the address or phone number of a well-established business or organization, or for the date or location of a well-publicized event. Librarians, of course, should be held to an even higher standard in this regard, since finding information is our business.

It is inconsiderate to assume that everyone has the same type of Internet access that you have. People who have free access to the Internet through work or school sometimes forget that other people pay by the message and/or by the minute. For example, there was an incident on the Trollope e-mail group when a member (perhaps inadvertently) e-mailed the full text of a Trollope novel to the whole group. This caused many list members to overrun disk quotas on their systems, incurring a charge and sometimes causing other mail to bounce.

Relevance is also an important concept in the online forums. Most readers have enough trouble keeping up with the relevant messages on various groups. When conversation strays off topic, private e-mail should be used. It is especially rude to try to use any pretext for sneaking in a little advertising, favorite political topics, etc. The proper use of subject lines is also important. Whether it's e-mail groups or USENET, subject lines should allow readers to choose messages of interest and delete the rest. Subject lines like "Help!" or "Question" or "A comment" are common but not helpful, because they don't indicate the subject of the posting.

CHANGING DEMOGRAPHICS

For many years, online communication was largely limited to young, technically-oriented men. This was true on both ends of the online spectrum, the Internet because of its connection to college and university computing departments, and the BBSs because of their association with the early home PC users. The commercial online systems, like America Online, CompuServe, and Prodigy, appealed to a more general, less technical crowd.

As the Internet has grown and developed, the online community has become much more diverse. As connections and interfaces have becomes simpler, the Internet has become a communication forum for everyone, not just for the technologically astute. Young people still represent a major force, partly due to their lifelong familiarity and comfort with computers and partly because so many colleges give all students free Internet access. However, other age groups are catching up, including the elderly, who find the online community decreases the sense of isolation that sometimes accompanies aging. Women have become increasingly active in all areas.

LIBRARIANS AND THE ONLINE WORLD

Librarians have always used a variety of methods for helping our patrons find the information they need. In addition to the books, journals, and other items owned by our libraries, we use community information and referral systems to find local organizations, and directories to find national organizations. We call the local consulate or newspaper or various agencies of local, state, or federal government. We maintain collections of maps and pamphlets and a wide variety of other sources of information. In order to maintain the library's role in the community, librarians need to be familiar and comfortable with online resources, on the Internet and beyond.

Popular subject areas are covered in many different forums on different systems. For example, there is a Genealogy BBS on Prodigy, Genealogy Club on America Online, Genealogy Forum on CompuServe, as well as conferences on FidoNet and RelayNet. In addition, there is a National Genealogical BBS sponsored by the National Genealogical Association that includes listings for other genealogical BBSs. On the Internet itself, there is a popular e-mail group called Roots-L, which is also available on USENET as the newsgroup soc.roots. Gopher and the World Wide Web have a number of sites devoted to genealogy. If we are working with genealogists, we need to be able to use some of these sources of information and provide referrals to our patrons, because if we limit ourselves to traditional sources, we are only doing half the job.

Both reference and collection development require us to be in touch with all types of information that our patrons might be seeking, and as the Internet continues to grow and develop as a forum for the exchange of information, librarians need to be actively involved in this new world, in order to keep fulfilling our traditional role as gatekeepers and guides to information resources.

NOTES

1. Coombs, Norman. "Your Onramp to the Internet: The Power of Electronic Mail." [World Wide Web] http://www.isc.rit.edu/~nrcgsh/tele/aahebc.95 (1 Feb 1996)
2. Eisenhood, Elizabeth. "Re: Hearing Impaired patrons." 14 Oct. 1995 [e-mail] AXSLIB-L@stjvm.stjohns.edu
3. Coombs, op. cit.
4. Eisenhood, op cit.
5. Coombs, op. cit.

2 TOOLS OF THE TRADE

Learning how to use the Internet presents some special problems. The Internet is not a system or a service. If your library buys a CD-ROM product, joins OCLC, or signs a contract for access to an online periodicals index, you have something new to learn, but that product or service is a single, defined system with one vendor who is responsible for providing some level of training, documentation, and support. The Internet, however, is much more complex, because it is inherently based on distributed processing, and distributed processing often means distributed problems. In order to be an effective Internet user, and to help solve your own problems, it is important to understand certain basic Internet tools, and to know how to use three essential services.

THE THREE ESSENTIALS: TRAINING, DOCUMENTATION, AND SUPPORT

I may be sitting at my desk using Netscape on my PC to access a World Wide Web site in England. If I keep getting an error, where's the problem? It could be a hardware or software problem on my PC, or something wrong in the way I have Windows configured. It could be a problem in the Netscape options; for example, I may not be seeing images because I have the Autoload images option turned off. It could be a problem on the network connecting my PC to my system's router, or in the phone line which connects that router to our Internet service provider, or their connection to the Internet. Of course, the problem may also be on the system in England.

Many of the problems and misunderstandings that people perceive as being "out on the Internet" are really close to home. The Internet is built on client/server technology, and to be an effective user, you need to understand the client programs that you are using. Reading Internet books, even this one, can't help you too much with this, because the authors don't know which client programs you are using and how your Internet access is set up.

PARTICIPATE IN TRAINING

As librarians, we are finding ourselves operating in a more and more complex environment, and our needs for training have increased dramatically over the last few years. Most libraries are having trouble providing staff with all the training that they need. Scheduling and desk coverage are as much of a problem as course and workshop fees.

Training is sometimes one of the hidden costs of automation, but allocating resources for training should be part of the planning for any new system or service. Lack of training is usually much more costly than training, if you consider all the time that people waste trying to use systems they don't understand, or the cost of straightening out mistakes caused by untrained users.

You should try to participate in as much training as you can. Notice that I said *participate* rather than *attend*. Know your own learning style. Some of us learn best by seeing, some by hearing, and some by doing. The best training session combines techniques, supplementing the spoken word with visual aids such as overheads and a chance to get your hands on the system to try things. Many librarians feel comfortable with classroom style training, but have a hard time with hands-on training and try to hide in the background for fear of making a mistake or looking foolish. These people ultimately miss some great opportunities to really learn a new system.

Whatever the format of the training, don't be afraid to ask questions. Librarians sometimes have a hard time with this, perhaps because we are generally in the business of providing answers for other people. Don't preface your questions by saying, "This is probably a stupid question . . . " Professional trainers will welcome questions and treat you with the same respect that you show patrons who ask you questions. Trainers know that for every person who asks a particular question, there are usually several other people sitting there wondering the same thing but afraid to ask.

READ THE DOCUMENTATION

There is no way to avoid this one although you may feel overwhelmed by the task. Software is complex, and to understand all its features, you need to read the documentation. This may be in the form of manuals or online help systems, or it may be in the form of memos or handouts from meetings and training sessions.

Reading the documentation probably won't answer all your questions or allow you to solve all of your own problems, but it may teach you some time-saving features that you never would have found on your own. The most important benefit of reading the documentation may be that when you do need help, you will be in a better position to explain your problem to the Systems Administrator.

SUPPORT: YOU'VE GOT A FRIEND

Get to know your local Systems Administrator. I am using this generic term to represent whoever is responsible for supporting your Internet use. Depending on your circumstances, this could be a single person whose title actually is Systems Administrator or something similar, or someone who manages the system in addition to other responsibilities. Systems support may be shared among a group of people, with training on resources and services often separate from hardware/software administration. If you are getting Internet access by dialing into a commercial Internet service provider, support may be in the form of a help desk or technical support phone number. The important thing is to make sure you know who is responsible for providing you with support, and how you can reach them.

Asking for help will provide you with the opportunity to practice the reference interview from the other side. Be prepared to explain your problem carefully, explaining just what you are trying to do and what problem you are having. Before you call, write down everything you think may be relevant, including any error messages. Troubleshooters are always trying to figure out where the problem is through a process of elimination, so it helps if you can identify when the problem occurs. For example, if the problem is with printing, can you print from other applications? If the problem is with connecting to a certain address through Netscape, can you connect to other addresses successfully? Can you connect to the same address through a different client, or from a different workstation?

An answer of an effective question would be "I am having a problem printing from Netscape. It prints half a page and then stops and ejects the page. It's an HP Laser Jet 520, and it is printing normally in Word and other applications. I looked at the printer configurations in Netscape and it seems to be configured correctly." "How come this stupid printer doesn't work?" is a poorly worded question, because it doesn't provide any information to help a technician diagnose your problem.

UNDERSTANDING YOUR CONNECTION TO THE INTERNET

Before we talk about some specific Internet services, you should make sure you understand a basic distinction between two types of Internet connection. The essential question is this: are you at a terminal or a computer?

You may be at a terminal that is connected to your library automation system, which has an Internet connection, or is connected to a computer that does. You may be connected to this system by cables within a single building, or by dedicated phone lines if the system is in another building, or you may dial up the system via a modem. In any case, you are logging into the host system and working on the host system's environment or operating system. If that system runs the UNIX operating system, you will be using a UNIX e-mail program like Elm or Pine, the UNIX Gopher client, and a UNIX World Wide Web browser like Lynx.

Your "terminal" may actually be a PC, running terminal emulation software. This may be the case if you have substituted a PC for a terminal connected to your library system, or if you are dialing into a shell account (a text-based account in which your computer emulates a dumb terminal, connects to an Internet host, and uses software on the Internet Service Provider's computer) with a commercial Internet service provider. Having a PC running as a terminal brings some advantages. You are probably connecting with a PC communication/terminal emulation program which will allow you to capture data that appears on the screen to a file, or to transfer files from the system to the PC using Kermit, Xmodem, Ymodem, or Zmodem. But you are still working on a terminal and limited to the software running on the host system.

The other possibility is that you are using a computer that is directly on the Internet. For example, your PC may be connected to a LAN (local area network) that has a direct Internet connection. Another possibility is that you are dialing into a commercial Internet service provider using a SLIP (Serial Line Internet Protocol) or PPP (Point to Point Protocol) account. These are protocols that make a connection that allows your PC to be (at least temporarily) a true computer on the Internet.

If you are using a computer on the Internet, you are working in your own operating system, for example, Windows instead of UNIX. You will have a choice of software to use, rather than being dependent on what was chosen for the host system. This means that you can use Netscape or Mosaic as a World Wide Web browser, for example.

These easy, powerful, graphical programs have helped make SLIP/PPP accounts popular, and have added a lot of incentive for systems to upgrade their telecommunication and network connections to support this level of access for PCs. The downside of being a "computer" rather than a "terminal" is the responsibility for acquiring, installing, learning, and troubleshooting network software on the local PC. Graphics files are also very large compared to text, and can cause problems for systems that were never designed or sized for this level of use. In library systems, it is especially important to protect the transmission of circulation data from slowdowns caused by graphics transfers.

These are the two basic scenarios, but things have gotten a little more complicated. There is now software such as SLIPknot, that allows a serial connection to impersonate a SLIP connection and transfer graphics to the PC. Further variations are sure to develop, as everyone has tried to raise their level of connectivity at the lowest possible cost. As the Internet has moved from a primarily text-based environment to include graphics, video, and sound, there is great pressure to get everyone, literally, up to speed. The technical details of how all of this works can be left to the techies, but it is helpful to have a basic understanding of the nature of your connection.

THE BASIC PROTOCOLS

The Internet is based on three protocols: e-mail, telnet, and FTP. These are often not used directly, but through a World Wide Web browser, but it helps to understand the nature of these underlying programs.

E-MAIL

E-mail is one of the three basic Internet protocols, and is still the most popular Internet activity. You use an e-mail program to compose and send messages, and to read and delete messages that are sent to you. There are many different e-mail programs available for different operating systems, and they all use different commands and provide different features. There are some general things you should know about how Internet e-mail works.

E-mail addresses follow the general form **user@host.domain**. The **user** part is your user name on your own system, generally the same user name that you use to log-in to the system. The **host.domain** part is the name of your system, and its domain, and there may be more than two parts to the address. Domain names follow two general patterns. Many systems in the United States are identified by a three-letter code indicating the type of site:

edu	Educational systems
org	Organizations
com	Commercial systems
net	Networks
gov	Government systems
mil	Military systems

Systems outside the United States, and newer systems within the United States, generally end with a two letter country code, for example:

us	United States
uk	United Kingdom
jp	Japan
de	Germany
[etc.]	

There are many variations possible, depending on how your system was set up. In addition, your system may be using an alias to give users a simpler e-mail address. For example, the e-mail address that I give people is et@noble.mass.edu. This means that I have an account in the user name et on the system of the organization called NOBLE, which is a subnetwork of a system called MASSNET, which is an educational system. However, if I send you e-mail, you will see my "true" e-mail address, which is et@clsn1102.noble.mass.edu. **Clsn1102** is the actual machine name of the system at NOBLE where my e-mail is directed. It's not necessary for this to be included in incoming mail, because the machine that receives NOBLE's mail knows which machine I'm on and directs the mail accordingly.

You can leave the details of this up to your Systems Administrator, but all users should know both their "easy" e-mail address, the version they can give out to colleagues, and their "true" e-mail address, the one that will be seen in mail headers. If you don't know your true e-mail address, just send yourself a message and look in the header. Knowing this will help you if the discrepancy in the address causes problems. You may be trying to unsubscribe from an e-mail list, for example, and get a message that you are not a member of the list, because it only reads your true address and you are using your "easy" version. In general, if you are sending commands to software, always use your true e-mail address so it will match the one in your mail header.

TELNET

Telnet is one of the oldest protocols of the Internet, and its basic purpose is to connect someone at one system to another system and act as a terminal on that system. Telnet has played a pivotal role for libraries by providing public access to library catalogs. In fact, when the Internet began to grow beyond the military and technical community, online library catalogs gained attention, since there weren't many other types of publicly available online systems.

Telnet is a useful, basic protocol for connecting to another system, whether it's your own system and you are logging in from elsewhere to check your e-mail, a system that allows public access through a generic log-in such as a library or catalog, or a commercial system that allows account holders access using their account number and password. However, telnet is a low-level protocol in terms of client/server, and is gradually becoming less important as the World Wide Web allows information to be passed between systems using the full power of the PC for an improved interface and display.

There are no specific commands to learn for telnet itself, other than how to enter a telnet command on your own system. This could be done through a menu or through another application. Typically, you would type the command **telnet [address]** at the basic prompt. Once the connection is made, you log in to the other system and are working in that system's environment. Once I log in to an online catalog, for example, I am using the same commands and search strategies that I would be using if I were at a terminal in the library.

FTP

FTP, or File Transfer Protocol, is another of the original, basic protocols of the Internet. FTP allows you to connect as a terminal on another system, move through the directories of that system, and retrieve or deposit files. The original intent of FTP was to allow known users with accounts on the system to have access to files. As the use of the Internet grew, however, Systems Managers began making certain directories available to the public, using the log-in name *anonymous*.

FTP was, and still is, a useful, direct method for moving files from one system to another, if someone has given you the system address, the path to the file, and the file name. It can be tricky, however, to navigate through the directories and subdirectories on another system, and FTP was never designed for browsing. As more sophisticated systems like Gopher and the World Wide Web developed, FTP has become increasingly a background protocol, used by systems to move files with the Gopher or World Wide Web client acting as an interface.

The following example shows a standard FTP session. I am connecting to the FTP server of the World, a public access UNIX system, to check out the cookie recipes that I have been told are available in the /obi/Recipes directory. The commands that I typed are printed in bold; all responses came from the World's server.

```
%ftp ftp.std.com
Connected to ftp.std.com.
220 ftp.std.com FTP server (Version wu-2.4(19) Thu Jul 6 21:54:21 HST
    1995) ready.
Name (ftp.std.com:et): anonymous
331 Guest login ok, send your complete e-mail address as password.
Password:
230-
230-Hello!
230-
230-This is the anonymous FTP area for world.std.com, a public access UNIX
230-system.
230-
230-Current local time in Brookline, MA is Sat Nov 11 16:19:18 1995.
230-Running with 97 (out of 450) ftp users.
230-
230-Accounts directly on the system are available via telnet at
230-world.std.com, or via direct-dial by calling 617-739-9753 (8N1,
230-V.32bis (14.4K), V.32 (9600), 2400) or 617-739-2300 (8N1, 28.8K).
230-Login as new (no password) to create an account. Accounts are charged
230-at $5/mo+$2/hr or $20/20hrs/month, your choice.
230-
230-Grab the details in the world-info directory here if interested.
230-
230-Contact staff@world.std.com if you encounter problems with this server!
230-
230-
230-Please read the file README
230-it was last modified on Sat Oct 22 11:14:48 1994 - 385 days ago
230 Guest login ok, access restrictions apply.
ftp> cd /obi/Recipes
250 CWD command successful.
ftp> dir
200 PORT command successful.
150 Opening ASCII mode data connection for /bin/ls.
total 28
drwxrwxr-x 2 obi src 1024 Sep 18 1991 appetizers
drwxrwxr-x 2 obi src 1024 Sep 18 1991 breads
drwxrwxr-x 2 obi src 1024 Sep 18 1991 casseroles
drwxrwxr-x 2 obi src 512 Sep 18 1991 cookies
drwxrwxr-x 2 obi src 2048 Sep 18 1991 desserts
drwxrwxr-x 2 obi src 512 Sep 18 1991 jewish
```

```
drwxrwxr-x 2 obi src 512 Sep 18 1991 lowcal
drwxrwxr-x 2 obi src 1024 Sep 18 1991 meats
drwxrwxr-x 2 obi src 512 Sep 18 1991 poultry
drwxrwxr-x 2 obi src 512 Sep 18 1991 salads
drwxrwxr-x 2 obi src 512 Sep 18 1991 seafood
drwxrwxr-x 2 obi src 512 Sep 18 1991 soups
drwxrwxr-x 2 obi src 512 Sep 18 1991 vegetables
226 Transfer complete.
675 bytes received in 0.45 seconds (1.46 Kbyte/s)
ftp> cd /obi/Recipes/cookies
250 CWD command successful.
ftp> dir
200 PORT command successful.
150 Opening ASCII mode data connection for /bin/ls.
total 28
-rw-rw-r— 1 obi src 500 Apr 5 1991 aebleskiver
-rw-rw-r— 1 obi src 619 Apr 5 1991 elephant
-rw-rw-r— 1 obi src 651 Apr 5 1991 finnpancakes
-rw-rw-r— 1 obi src 567 Apr 5 1991 ginger
-rw-rw-r— 1 obi src 483 Apr 5 1991 krumkake
-rw-rw-r— 1 obi src 662 Apr 5 1991 lemonsquares
-rw-rw-r— 1 obi src 623 Apr 5 1991 matrimony
-rw-rw-r— 1 obi src 938 Apr 5 1991 mochanut
-rw-rw-r— 1 obi src 532 Apr 5 1991 poppyseed
-rw-rw-r— 1 obi src 671 Apr 5 1991 rangers
-rw-rw-r— 1 obi src 634 Apr 5 1991 rosemarysq
-rw-rw-r— 1 obi src 933 Apr 5 1991 rugelach
-rw-rw-r— 1 obi src 797 Apr 5 1991 shortbread
-rw-rw-r— 1 obi src 448 Apr 5 1991 swedspritz
226 Transfer complete.
740 bytes received in 0.67 seconds (1.08 Kbyte/s)
ftp> get shortbread
200 PORT command successful.
150 Opening ASCII mode data connection for shortbread (797 bytes).
226 Transfer complete.
local: shortbread remote: shortbread
813 bytes received in 0.23 seconds (3.45 Kbyte/s)
ftp> quit
221 Goodbye.
%
```

First I use the command **ftp** and the system's address, I log in as anonymous and give my e-mail address as the password. At the **ftp>** prompt, I enter the **cd** command and the path to the directory: **cd /obi/Recipes**. At the next **ftp>** prompt, I enter the command **dir** to list the contents of the directory. There I find a listing for "cookies," which I can see is a directory from the first letter of the line— a little UNIX knowledge is needed here. I use the **cd** command to switch to the cookies directory, and the **dir** command to list the contents of that directory. I see a file listed for shortbread, and I use the **get** command to transfer it to my home system.

There are really only a few commands you need to know to do anonymous FTP:

cd [path]	Change directory
dir	List contents of a directory
get [filename]	Transfer file
quit	Exit the system

However, FTP is an old and unfriendly program, and many people try it once, fail, and give up. It's worth learning because once you get past the awkwardness, it's the most direct way to get files that you want, assuming you know where they are.

THE FOUR MOST COMMON MISTAKES IN ANONYMOUS FTP

1. Spelling **anonymous** wrong. People get so nervous about their upcoming battles with directories and filenames that they spell incorrectly.
2. Typos in directories or file names. Copy these carefully, and be especially careful about capitalization, since UNIX is case-sensitive. In this example, the path to my file is **/obi/Recipes/cookies**, which, to UNIX, is entirely different from **/obi/recipes/cookies**.
3. Slashes. People with a lot of DOS experience often type directories as **\obi\Recipes\cookies**. UNIX directories use the backslash (/) not the forward slash (\).
4. Mistaking a file for a directory, or a directory for a file. People try to do the **dir** command on a file or the **get** command on a directory. You can learn a little UNIX, or, when in doubt about whether something is a file or a directory, do the **dir** command and see.

The example I have just shown is classic UNIX FTP. If, however, you have access to a graphical World Wide Web browser such as Netscape, you have a much better alternative. Using Netscape, I can open the URL ftp://ftp.std.com/obi/Recipes/ and use the browser as an interface.

Here we see the same directory listing, but Netscape can recognize what is a directory and displays these with file folder icons. I can move through the directory structure by pointing and clicking, and I don't need to know commands or transcribe paths or file names.

FIGURE 2.1 Using Netscape as an Interface for FTP

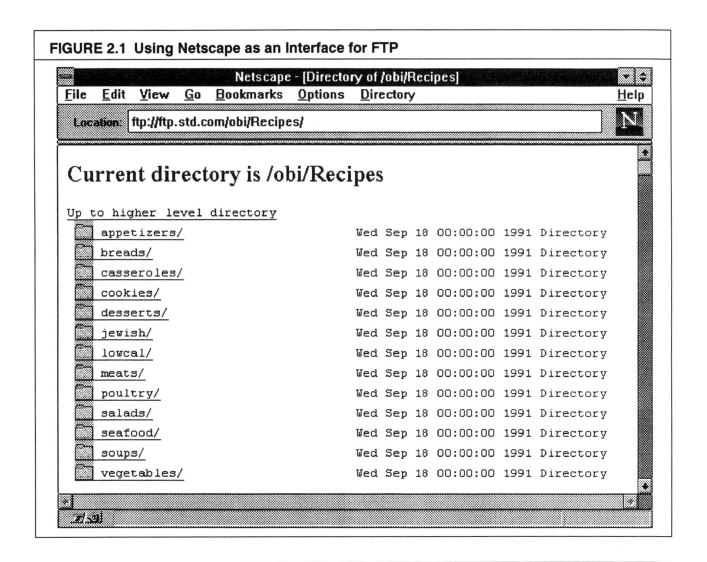

WAIS: WIDE AREA INFORMATION SERVERS

WAIS in an indexing and retrieval system designed by Brewster Kahle and a collaboration between Thinking Machines, Dow Jones, Apple Computers, and KPMC Peat Marwick. WAIS is designed to index large, full-text databases, and like almost everything on the Internet, works on the client/server model. The idea was to install a WAIS client on your own machine, and use it to access a complete list of WAIS databases called the Directory of Servers. You would then select one or more databases, construct a search, and send it to the server to retrieve matching records.

Now, however, you are far more likely to run into WAIS indirectly, as searchable databases on Gophers or the World Wide Web. WAIS software is freely available for many different types of computers, and has become the de facto indexing standard of the Internet. If you run into a search form on Gopher or the Web, you can generally assume that it's WAIS.

WAIS works well for searching full text databases, such as collections of speeches, articles, papers, and the archives of e-mail groups. The search strategy is different from the bibliographic searching that most of us know from online catalogs and periodicals indexes. With a WAIS database, you enter a group of search terms, which the server matches against the database. The WAIS software then assigns a score to each match, with 1,000 as the best match. Records above a certain score are displayed, in descending order, with the most relevant records first. The scores are based on the number of search terms that appear in the record, and the number of times that each term appears. Less weight is given to common words.

The best way to search a WAIS database is to use three or more terms, rather than only one or two relevant terms, and to try to avoid very common words. An example would be searching with the terms "French" and "dessert" and "cake" rather than simply using cake. Different versions of WAIS have somewhat different search rules, and, if you are lucky, there will be information about the database and how it can be searched. If there isn't, experiment with a few different searches to see how a particular database works.

URLS: UNIFORM RESOURCE LOCATORS

URLs are a system of notation for all types of Internet connections. This system is an easy, precise shorthand, similar to the way we exchange phone numbers. When I give you my phone number in the format (000) 000–0000, I assume that you know how to dial that number, whether or not you need to use the area code, and won't try to dial the parentheses and hyphen. Internet addresses may be given in prose: "To connect to the catalog, telnet to public.noble.mass.edu, and log-in as library, no password needed" or "Point your Gopher client to gopher.noble.mass.edu." URL provides an alternative, uniform shorthand for conveying that information, just like phone numbers use a standard format.

The URL generally consists of three parts: the protocol, the

Figure 2.2 WAIS Results by Score

```
                                    Search of eric-digests (p3 of 5)
   + ED340148 Nov 91 Developing Effective Programs for Special
     Education Students Who Are Homeless. E" Date: 00/00/00
     Score: 716, Lines: 195, Bytes: 10947

          TEXT

   + ED315865 89 Coping with Changing Demographics. ERIC Digest
     Series Number EA45. Date: 00/00/00 Score: 647, Lines: 206,
     Bytes: 10152

          TEXT

   + ED338745 Jun 91 Highly Mobile Students: Educational Problems
     and Possible Solutions. ERIC/CUE Di" Date: 00/00/00 Score:
     590, Lines: 193, Bytes: 10256

          TEXT

   + ED345929 Mar 92 Changing Schools through Experiential
     Education. ERIC Digest. Date: 00/00/00 Score: 578, Lines:
 -- press space for next page --
  Arrow keys: Up and Down to move. Right to follow a link; Left to go back.
 H)elp O)ptions P)rint G)o M)ain screen Q)uit /=search [delete]=history list
```

address, and the path. The **protocol** is the type of resource or, more accurately, the method of connection. The most common protocols that you will see in URLs are telnet, gopher, FTP (file transfer protocol) and HTTP (hypertext transfer protocol). The protocol is followed by a colon and two slashes. The **address** is the location of the system where the resource is found, and the **path** is the location of the resource on the system. Different types of URLs have additional information, for example, a telnet URL has the log-in information before the address, followed by a @ sign. For example, **telnet://library@public.noble.mass.edu.**

The URL may be used in two ways. Many people are using a World Wide Web browser or other software that allows them to enter the URL directly to make a connection. Others can use the URL to get the information they need to make their own connection. If I am using a shell account on a public UNIX system, for example, **telnet://library@public.noble.mass.edu** means I should type **telnet public.noble.mass.edu** and log-in as **library.**

HAVE YOUR CLIENT CALL MY CLIENT...

Using Netscape to do FTP points to a general fact of life on the Internet. In the old days (which in Internet terms means about five years ago) Internet access was limited to those willing to learn unfriendly, mostly UNIX, client programs for e-mail, telnet, FTP, and USENET news. Those client programs have now been largely eclipsed by more complex but friendlier programs, and integrated suites of programs.

These new client programs are easier to use than their UNIX predecessors, but bring their own complexities. When Internet access was through terminals or PCs emulating terminals, all of the client software was on the host machine, and the problem for users was learning how to work with those programs. Now, the client programs are typically on your own desktop computer, and your biggest problem is acquiring, installing, and managing all that software, and troubleshooting the inevitable problems.

As client programs become more complex, users have a variety of options, which is generally a good thing. For example, you can read USENET news using a newsreader program, such as trn or tin, but you can also read and post to USENET through an e-mail program, such as Pine, or a World Wide Web browser, such as Netscape, provided it has been configured for this. There are many client programs that rely on other client programs to perform various functions, and this can cause confusion.

Suppose you wanted to have your kitchen renovated. This is a job that involves both carpentry and plumbing. You can hire a carpenter and plumber separately, or you can hire a carpenter, who will subcontract with a plumber, or you can hire a plumber, who will subcontract with a carpenter. Client programs work the same way. You may be using Netscape or another World Wide Web browser, but when you reach a telnet connection, Netscape needs to call up a telnet client to make the connection. You may be using Gopher, but when you reach a Gopher link to a World Wide Web page, Gopher needs to have a World Wide Web browser configured for its use. When you move beyond text, you need special programs to handle graphics and sound files. Your primary client may bring you to many resources and then fail, because it is missing helper applications.

This brings us back to training, documentation, and support. You need to find out which applications you can and can't do with your favorite client programs, not just which applications those programs are technically capable of supporting. For that you need to communicate with your local systems people or Internet access providers, and to read your documentation.

TAKING THE TIME TO LEARN

Librarians are increasingly pressed for time. We feel pressure to learn so many new things in a rapidly changing environment, while we continue to provide traditional service. We are constantly trying to balance our responsibility to provide service to the patron who comes to the library today with our need to learn new skills to help the patron who may come in tomorrow.

It's a constant balancing act, and one that is not likely to improve anytime in the near future. Training takes time, but lack of training leads to ineffective use of resources and wasted time. There is needed information for your patrons on the Internet, if only you can find it. People are participating in discussions of books about every possible subject, which provides invaluable information for collection development, if only you can tap into this exchange. Taking the time to learn how to use new tools effectively can help you provide better guidance and service to all of your patrons, today and tomorrow.

E-MAIL GROUPS

E-mail was invented to allow people to send messages from one computer to another. The original intent was to allow electronic memos to be sent from one individual to another, or from one individual to several others who were part of the same work group. However, it didn't take computer users long to figure out how to use e-mail to form discussion groups. E-mail groups are the oldest social institution on the Internet.

The concept of e-mail groups developed quickly, on both the Internet and the BITNET, the academic e-mail network. There are now e-mail groups devoted to a wide variety of personal and professional interests, including many different aspects of librarianship. Reference and collection development librarians can use professional e-mail groups to communicate with each other, and can use other groups to tap into the collective knowledge and information sharing on various subjects.

HOW THE E-MAIL GROUPS WORK

E-mail groups operate on mailing lists, just like magazines and mail order catalogs, except, of course, that the addresses are e-mail addresses rather than postal addresses. Postal mailing lists only work in one direction—a company can send out 1,000 copies of its catalog at once, but there is no easy way for a recipient to send an opinion to everyone else who received the catalog. Most Internet mailing lists are two-way; however, some mailing lists are one-way, like postal mailing lists. These are the distribution lists for electronic journals, software updates, or membership notices. But the kind of mailing lists we are discussing in this chapter are two-way. Messages are sent out to all members of the list, and messages may be sent in reply to all members of the list.

The communication on an e-mail group often has an intense, immediate quality that can't be matched. For example, when Cynthia Ozick's "Rediscovery" article on Anthony Trollope appeared on the front page of the *New York Times Book Review*, several messages critiquing the article were posted to a Trollope e-mail group within hours, setting off a lively discussion on a number of points made in the article. Without the e-mail group, how could Trollope-lovers have reacted to this article? Those who had Trollope-loving friends could have called them to discuss it; academics could have discussed it among their colleagues; and others would have no recourse but to write a letter to the *Times* or wait for the next meeting of the local Trollope Society. Having a group of people who share the same interest instantly available to you whenever you need to ask a question, make a comment, or pass along a piece of relevant news is one of the best things about the e-mail groups.

Discussion lists vary in style, tone, and content. Some, especially the professional groups, tend to be somewhat formal in tone, with messages that are written almost as carefully as letters to the editor. Other groups are informal, chatty, personal, and digressive. The number of messages, known as the amount of traffic, on the groups varies as well. Some groups average only one or two messages a week, while other may have fifty or more messages a day. A comfortable traffic level for most people is somewhere in the range of two to ten messages a day. This is enough for the group to be engaging but not so many that a few days of unchecked mail presents an overwhelming volume of messages.

E-mail groups have a feeling of intensity because everyone receives all the messages from the group, and most members read, or at least scan, every message. This creates a sense of shared experience, and members will often refer to earlier discussions. In almost every group, there are a few prominent members who post frequent messages and seem endlessly willing to share their expertise, or to suggest new topics when the discussion is flagging. There will also be a corps of members who post occasionally, jumping in whenever their special area of interest comes up. Beyond this, there are large numbers of lurkers, people who never post anything but just monitor the discussion.

Most lists form a sense of community that allows them to stay together through the disputes and disagreements that inevitably strike most groups. Every subject has certain areas of controversy, and by definition the people who join e-mail groups care deeply about their subject. In every group, there will be a constant exchange of views, including polite disagreements, all the time, with occasional outbursts that transcend the bounds of polite discourse. This reflects the intensity that successful e-mail groups attain, and the relative ease of firing off a reply.

E-mail makes it easy, sometimes too easy, to send a message to scores of people simultaneously. With postal mail, you have to produce the letter, find an envelope, find a stamp, and mail the letter. Each action gives you a minute or two to calm down and rethink the wisdom of sending the message. With e-mail, the message can be composed and sent and distributed around the globe in a matter of minutes. Most groups, however, transcend these disagreements. There are usually a few peacemakers on the group, who will send messages acknowledging that both sides in a dispute have some merit, that the discussion has been enlightening, and that perhaps it is time to agree to disagree and move on to a new topic.

E-mail groups often bring together diverse groups of people who may not share many characteristics except for their love of canaries or knitting or science fiction or whatever is the topic of the group. On the literary and historical groups, for example, there are many graduate students and college faculty members who bring a wealth of information to the group, along with other people in many different fields who simply have a deep personal interest in the writings of Charlotte Brontë or the Civil War or the Middle Ages. Those in this second group who have a love for their subject may be called "amateurs" in the truest sense of the word. The amateurs benefit from the expertise of the professionals, and the professionals benefit from the honest enthusiasm and different perspective of the amateurs.

LIST MANAGEMENT

E-mail groups or lists are sometimes called *Listservs*, taking the name of the list management software commonly used on the BITNET. Listserv is more than list management software; it is also, in effect, a network of lists running on systems that are linked, that know about each other, and that can process shared commands. For example, sending the **command list global** to a Listserv machine will retrieve the complete list of BITNET e-mail groups. The fact that all these lists use the same software and the same sets of commands and conventions is also helpful for list members, who can learn the basic commands for subscribing, signing off, setting list options, etc., and apply this knowledge to many groups.

However, adopting the specific term Listserv to the more general world of e-mail groups presents some problems, as users try to send Listserv commands to groups that are managed by other types of software or manually. An e-mail group, technically, consists of two simple pieces : a file that is a list of e-mail addresses, and an alias that directs mail sent to the list name to be sent to every address in that file. Small, stable e-mail lists can be maintained easily by hand, with someone taking the responsibility to edit the list file to add and delete addresses as needed.

Adding and deleting e-mail addresses from a file, however, is just the sort of task that computers perform well, and a variety of list management software packages are now in use, along with individual, simple, homegrown scripts. Some common types of list management software include Majordomo and Listproc. It usually doesn't matter to the members what type of list management software, if any, is being used. All you really need to do is to follow the directions for joining a group. This is something that should be done slowly, carefully, and exactly. When you join a list, you will usually receive a welcome message that will include basic information about the list including the instructions for unsubscribing. Save this message, either by printing it out or storing it as a file or in a mail folder; you will need it later.

The worst (and most common) error that you can make with list management software is to confuse the list management address and the address of the list itself. Subscription requests and other list management details (known as administrivia) should never be sent to the list address. If they are, they will either be distributed to all the members of the group, who will be annoyed to receive this extraneous mail and can't help you anyway, or it will bounce to the listowner/moderator, causing extra work, which is also not the best way to join a group. The list address usually has a descriptive, meaningful name, like BLUES-L or TWAIN-L or VEGGIE. (The true Listserv lists often use the "-L" convention for naming e-mail lists.) These addresses should be used for messages intended for the whole group, not for administrative purposes. The list management address is usually the name of the list management software, such as Listserv or Majordomo, or is in the form "listname-request."

Every group is using the disk space and facilities of a host site. Sometimes this support is donated by the system, as in the case of the Listserv groups sponsored and supported by universities. In other cases, individuals run e-mail groups at their own expense, using the facilities of commercial Internet service providers. Each group has a listowner who is responsible for handling the administration of the group, and who may step in from time to time to resolve problems.

Lists may be *moderated* or *unmoderated*. In a moderated group, all messages are checked by the moderator before being passed along to the group. Members sometimes see this as editorial control or even censorship, but most moderators only weed out misaddressed administrative messages and messages that are clearly inappropriate for the group. In an unmoderated group, all messages are sent directly to the group without intervention. Lists may be *private*, in which case only messages from members of the group can be posted to the group. This is becoming more common, as a way to prevent spamming (sending unwanted messages to multiple Listservs.)

There are a number of other options that may be available for each group, depending on the list management software and the options that have been chosen. Options include the ability to retrieve a list of members of the group, the choice of having the mail sent as a digest, or one long e-mail message, instead of as individual e-mail messages, and the ability to search and retrieve messages from the group archives. The welcome message that you receive when you join the group will usually explain what options are available and what commands to use.

SUBSCRIBING AND UNSUBSCRIBING : LISTSERV

Listserv is still the predominant list management software, and all Listserv lists use the same commands. Other list management software often uses commands patterned after Listserv.

The request to join a group managed by Listserv is :

SUBSCRIBE [LISTNAME] [YOURNAME].

This means that you send the command SUBSCRIBE followed by the name of the list. The name of the list is necessary because the Listserv address at one site may be managing hundreds of different lists.

The last part of the command, your name, is there for the purpose of the directory or list of subscribers that Listserv maintains. Your name will appear in this list next to your e-mail address, and this list can be retrieved by anyone sending the REVIEW [LISTNAME] command to the list. Your name should be in natural order here, first name first, in whatever format you prefer, including initials, title, etc. Sometimes people follow the instructions too closely and use quotation marks, brackets, or other symbols that were used in instructions. I have also seen people who followed the instructions so closely that they are forever listed in directories as FIRSTNAME LASTNAME.

Notice in that last example that I never told the Listserv my e-mail address. This is because the software takes the address from the message header. This gives the list your real address, which may not be the form of address that you use every day. Many systems use aliases to give users shorter, easier forms of address.

Here's what my subscription message to join the Victorian Studies list, VICTORIA, would look like:

FIGURE 3.1 Subscription Message Sent to VICTORIA

To: listserv@iubvm.ucs.indiana.edu
Subject:
SUBSCRIBE VICTORIA Elizabeth B. Thomsen

When I send this message, I will receive back two messages; one is a welcome message with more information about the group. This message is one that I should keep. If you are using an e-mail program with folders, you might want to create a folder called *lists* and use it for the welcome messages and updates from any lists you join. This makes it easy to find them when you need to unsubscribe to everything at once, for example, when you are changing jobs, or when your e-mail address changes. The second message is a brief report of list resources used, which looks like this:

FIGURE 3.2 Resource Message from VICTORIA

Date: Sun, 30 Jul 1995 19:00:59 -0500
From: "L-Soft list server at IUBVM (1.8b)"
            <LISTSERV@IUBVM.UCS.INDIANA.EDU>
To: Elizabeth Thomsen <et@CLSN1102.NOBLE.MASS.EDU>
Subject: Output of your job "et"

> SUBSCRIBE VICTORIA Elizabeth B. Thomsen
You have been added to the VICTORIA list.

Summary of resource utilization

CPU time:	2.761 sec	Device I/O:	115
Overhead CPU:	0.300 sec	Paging I/O:	6
CPU model:	7470	DASD model:	3370

Listserv sends you messages like this for everything, and you can just delete them.

To leave the list, I would send the command SIGNOFF [LISTNAME] to the Listserv address :

FIGURE 3.3 Signoff Message Sent to VICTORIA
To:listserv@iubvm.ucs.indiana.edu Subject: SIGNOFF VICTORIA

Notice that you don't need to include your name to this message. Listserv removes you from the e-mail list based on the e-mail address in your return address.

SUBSCRIBING AND UNSUBSCRIBING: OTHER TYPES OF LISTS

Lists running on software other than Listserv use similar commands with slight (but important) variations. The important thing is to follow directions carefully. For example, to join the Bronte discussion list, running on Majordomo software, you would send the following message :

FIGURE 3.4 Subscription Message Sent to Bronte
To: majordomo@world.std.com Subject: SUBSCRIBE BRONTE

Note that in this case you would not add your name, because the Majordomo software does not use this for the directory the way that Listserv does. What Majordomo expects to see after the listname, if anything, is an e-mail address. When it receives information that it doesn't understand, it bounces the message to the listowner, who will send commands to process the request. This causes more work for the listowner and a delay for the potential subscriber.

There are other lists that need the subscribe command in a different format, or even in the subject line rather than the body of the e-mail message. There are also groups that are maintained by hand. The standard Internet convention for such groups is to use an address in the form *listname-request* for list management messages. This address would be monitored by a human, who would read messages sent in any format and make the needed changes to the list. A message to join such a group would look like this :

FIGURE 3.5 Subscription Message Sent to Ballroom

To:ballroom-request@world.std.com
Subject:
Please add me to the ballroom list. Thank you.

Elizabeth B. Thomsen
et@noble.mass.edu

REPLYING TO LISTS

When you are responding to messages sent to a list, you should be careful where your response is being sent. Lists may be configured in a few different ways. For some lists, the "From" line is the list itself, and for others, it is the original sender. Many lists use the "Reply To:" line in the header for the list address. For example, here is a message from the VICTORIA list. The sender of this message was responding to a message called "Valentines in novels," and her e-mail program used the standard "Re:" format for the subject line of the response. If I wanted to respond to this message, I would need to distinguish between the "From:" line and the "Reply to" line, which is the group. Some e-mail software prompts you for this choice and some don't. The important thing is to check the header of your responses carefully so you know where your response is going, and to edit the header as necessary.

FIGURE 3.6 Message to VICTORIA, with "From" and "Reply to" Fields

From apease@AZTEC.CO.ZA
Date: Wed, 2 Aug 1995 08:55:00 EET
From: Allison Pease <apease@AZTEC.CO.ZA>
Reply to: VICTORIA 19th-Century British Culture & Society
   <VICTORIA@IUBVM.UCS.INDIANA.EDU>
To: Multiple recipients of list VICTORIA
<VICTORIA@IUBVM.UCS.INDIANA.EDU>
Subject: Re: Valentines in novels

This is probably obvious, but there is the Valentine that Batsheba sends to
Boldwood in Hardy's *Far From the Madding Crowd*.

Allison Pease
apease@aztec.co.za

The problem is that sometimes you want to send a response to a message to the list in order to participate in the discussion, and sometimes you want to send a response just to the sender of the message. It's good practice, in fact, to just send the message to the sender if you only want to tell her you agree with her ("Me too" messages) or if you want to send a personal followup not of general interest to the group. Sending these messages directly to an individual helps keep the number of list messages at a manageable level.

The real potential for embarrassment here is that you accidentally send a message to the group that was private and intended for the individual alone. This happens occasionally, especially when you see messages on a list from someone you know personally. Always study those message headers, especially the "Reply to" line in the incoming message.

MORE ABOUT LISTSERV

In addition to handling subscription options, Listserv can provide some other useful services. All communication with a Listserv may be done through e-mail, by sending messages that contain commands. The subject line should be left blank, and the syntax of the command must be exact. One Listserv may be maintaining many different lists, so be sure to include the list name where noted. Do not use signature files, or add other messages (or words like please and thank you) to commands because the software does not know how to interpret the extraneous characters. If you need to communicate with a person about the list, send a message to the moderator or list owner.

Please note : not all e-mail lists are running on Listserv software. The following information should be generally true of lists that are running on Listserv. The best source of information about a list is whatever you receive from the list itself.

LIST ARCHIVES

Many Listserv lists maintain archives in the form of monthly log files. Some lists also make available bibliographies and other useful files.

To retrieve a list of an available file, send a message to the Listserv address, with the command INDEX <LISTNAME> Example:

FIGURE 3.7 INDEX Command Sent to KIDLIT-L

To: listserv@bingvmb.cc.binghamton.edu
Subject:
INDEX KIDLIT-L

Here's the beginning of the message I would receive in response to the INDEX command.

FIGURE 3.8 INDEX from KIDLIT-L

```
Date:        Sun, 17 Sep 1995 15:05:00 +0000
From:        BITNET list server at BINGVM <LISTSERV@BINGVMB.cc.binghamton.edu>
To:          Elizabeth Thomsen <et@CLSN1102.NOBLE.MASS.EDU>
Subject:     File: "KIDLIT-L FILELIST"


*  KIDLIT-L FILELIST for LISTSERV@BINGVMB.
*
*  Archives for list KIDLIT-L (Children and Youth Literature List)
*
*  ...................................................
*
*  The GET/PUT authorization codes shown with each file entry describe
*  who is authorized to GET or PUT the file:
*
*    ALL = Everybody
*    OWN = List owners
*
*  ...................................................
*
*  NOTEBOOK archives for the list
*  (Monthly notebook)
*                 rec         last - change
* filename filetype  GET PUT -fm lrecl nrecs  date    time  Remarks
* _____ _____  ___ ___ ___ _____ _____ _____ _____ _____

   KIDLIT-L LOG9407ALL OWN V   80  5166 94/07/29 13:14:17 Started on Fri, 1 Jul 1994
08:06:16 ECT
   KIDLIT-L LOG9408ALL OWN V   80  3895 94/08/31 15:29:27 Started on Tue, 9 Aug 1994
13:22:40 ECT
   KIDLIT-L LOG9409ALL OWN V   80  5954 94/09/29 20:41:30 Started on Thu, 1 Sep 1994
08:47:46 ECT
   KIDLIT-L LOG9410ALL OWN V   80  3867 94/10/31 17:15:04 Started on Tue, 4 Oct 1994
15:23:31 ECT
```

To retrieve a file from the list, send a message to the Listserv address, with the command GET <FILENAME> <FILETYPE>. The filename and filetype are taken from the index file. The format of the list is awkward, but all you need to note is that monthly logs are available, and they are called KIDLIT-L LOG9507, with the digits after LOG representing the year and month.
Example:

FIGURE 3.9 File Request Sent to KIDLIT-L

To: listserv@bingvmb.cc.binghamton.edu
Subject:
GET KIDLIT-L LOG9407

Searching Archived Lists

If a list is archived, you can send a keyword search to the Listserv address to retrieve messages containing the words you specify. This can be very useful if you are trying to find something that you (or a patron) remembers having seen discussed on the list, or if you want to post a question about something but you want to see if it has already been discussed. It can also be a useful reference trick, if you are looking for a bit of information that may have been discussed on the list in the past. Retrieving the right messages can give you the information you need, or provide a useful clue on where to look.

To send a keyword search to the list, send the following message to the Listserv address :

```
//
database search dd=rules
//rules dd *
search <KEYWORD> in <LISTNAME>
print all
/*
```

Example:

FIGURE 3.10 Database Search Sent to AUSTEN-L

To: listserv@vm1.mcgill.ca
Subject:
```
//
database search dd=rules
//rules dd *
search Fanny Burney in AUSTEN-L
print all
/*
```

Because the form of message is so difficult to remember and hard to copy accurately, keyword searching of Listserv archives is one of the most underused Internet resources. If you learn how to do this effectively, it can be a great time-saver. Depending on how your system is configured, you can probably save the basic search as a file or template so you just have to enter the search term and the list name, and not remember the cryptic commands.

If you want to be more selective, you can replace the line "print all" with the word "index". This will retrieve a numbered list of messages, with dates and subject lines. You can then send the search again, replacing the line "print all" with "print all of <message#> <message#> <message#>".

Advanced Search Options

You can also specify a particular date range by adding "from yy/mm/dd to yy/mm/dd" to the end of the search line. Example :

FIGURE 3.11 Database Search with Date Range

```
To: listserv@vm1.mcgill.ca
Subject:
//
database search dd=rules
//rules dd *
search Fanny Burney in AUSTEN-L from 94/01/01 to 94/06/30
print all
/*
```

When you use two or more words, the Boolean operator AND is implied, and both words must be in a message for it to be considered a match. You can also use the Boolean operators OR and NOT.

Archives for Other Lists

Many non-Listserv lists also maintain archives. The best way to find these and learn how to search them is to read the welcome or information file for the group. For more information, you can contact the list owner, whose e-mail address should be listed in the welcome message you received when you joined the group. E-mail addressed to **listname-owner** usually also gets directed to the list owner. For example, if you wanted to send a message to the list owner of the list **bronte@world.std.com**, you could address it to **bronte-owner@world.std.com**.

Some e-mail groups maintain their archives on the Gopher or

World Wide Web site of their home system. For example, both PUBLIB, the public libraries discussion list, and PUBYAC, the Young Adult and Children's Services list, have their searchable archives available through the Gopher of NYSERNET, their home site, as well as through the usual Listserv commands.

To locate archives for a particular group, you can use Veronica to search Gophers, or a World Wide Web search engine such as Lycos, discussed in Chapter 7, which should turn up archives that are available on Gophers or Web sites. But again, the welcome message that you get when you join a group should be the first place to check for this kind of information.

LIBRARIANS AND THE LISTS

Many librarians participate in STUMPERS, PACS-L, PUBLIB, and other e-mail lists that are devoted to various aspects of librarianship, and many also participate in lists that are related to their personal interests. But there are also opportunities for librarians to use the various subject-oriented groups as a reference tool.

This needs to be done with care. The e-mail groups, far more than the USENET newsgroups, have a sense of belonging and membership. Because the messages from the group are sent to the members' e-mail boxes, they must be read or at least waded through and deleted on a regular basis. There is some burden belonging to an e-mail group, far more so than reading USENET. Messages from outsiders, who haven't, in effect, paid their dues, are not always well-received. It is particularly offensive to post a question, ending with something like, "Please send replies to me personally, since I am not a member of this list." This is like saying, "Send the messages to me personally, because I don't have time to be bothered participating in e-mail groups like all of you, unless, of course, I want something."

However, as people who are seeking help on behalf of others, librarians are in a better position to drop in on a group and ask for help. A polite message to a relevant group, asking a specific question on behalf of a patron, is generally well-received. The message should identify you as a librarian and briefly note what standard sources and other approaches have already been tried. This can work very well, since the questions that have stumped librarians are apt to be the sort of obscure detail that the aficionados on the group love answering.

E-mail groups also provide useful information for collection development. Books related to each group's topic are frequently discussed and sometimes hotly debated. Many questions posted to groups are somewhat beyond the scope of what can be adequately explained on e-mail, and so will be answered with a brief explanation and a reference to a book. If you are looking for some honest opinions on the relative merits of two new books on a subject, or for recommendations for the best books on a subject, posting a request to an e-mail group will quickly gather some frank and interesting results. Such messages are usually very welcome, as every group is anxious in encouraging an interest in their subject. In fact, you may get a lot of responses about the inadequacy of library collections on the group's topic.

With either reference or collection development requests, it's a good idea to join the group, post the question, wait for answers, post a message expressing appreciation, and then unsubscribe from the group. With the speed of e-mail traffic and the level of activity of most groups, this usually can all be accomplished in a few days. If there have been several messages posted, or replies sent to you privately, it's very helpful if you post a message that summarizes the responses received.

With reference questions, librarians are often concerned with what type of answer they would receive from strangers over the Internet. Librarians, of course, prefer answers to come with complete citations to reputable published works. The e-mail group members may not provide you with that, but can often provide helpful information or interpretations that can lead you to the answer in a published source. In fact, list members are often able to point out misinformation that has appeared in print, leading to confusion. The e-mail group has a self-regulatory function that helps provide accuracy. If one member posts the wrong answer, six others will quickly provide a correction.

The following examples are all related to Victorian literature, but demonstrate the general principles of using e-mail groups to get answers to questions.

E-mail groups tap into the collective experience and memory of a group of people who share a certain interest. These collective experiences can be a great help when you have a patron who is not looking for a single, definitive answer to a question, but who is looking for ideas, examples, or leads. For example, the following message was sent to VICTORIA, an e-mail group devoted to Victorian life and literature:

```
┌─────────────────────────────────────────────────────────────┐
│ FIGURE 3.12 Information Request on VICTORIA                  │
├─────────────────────────────────────────────────────────────┤
│ Date:      Tue, 1 Aug 1995  14:14:01  -0600                 │
│ From:      Britt Salvesen <bsalvesen@ARTIC.EDU>             │
│ Reply to:  VICTORIA 19th-Century British Culture & Society  │
│            <VICTORIA@IUBVM.UCS.INDIANA.EDU>                 │
│ To:        Multiple recipients of list VICTORIA             │
│            <VICTORIA@IUBVM.UCS.INDIANA.EDU>                 │
│ Subject:  Valentines in novels                             │
│ I am looking for references in Victorian literature (novels in particular, │
│ since I've got lots of poems) to Valentines.  Anything that describes │
│ Valentine cards themselves or the social rituals associated with their │
│ exchange would be greatly appreciated.                      │
│                                                             │
│ Britt Salvesen                                              │
│ bsalvesen@artic.edu                                         │
└─────────────────────────────────────────────────────────────┘
```

Within a few days, there were a number of responses, including the following :

FIGURE 3.13 Responses on VICTORIA

From wwmorgan@RS6000.CMP.ILSTU.EDUSun Aug 6 11:14:07 1995
Date: Wed, 2 Aug 1995 12:21:42 -0500
From: "William W. Morgan" <wwmorgan@RS6000.CMP.ILSTU.EDU>
Reply to: VICTORIA 19th-Century British Culture & Society <VICTORIA@IUBVM.UCS.INDIANA.EDU>
To: Multiple recipients of list VICTORIA <VICTORIA@IUBVM.UCS.INDIANA.EDU>
Subject: Re: Valentines in novels

I suppose someone will already have pointed out Bathsheba's ill-fated Valentine greeting to Boldwood in Hardy's Far From the Madding Crowd, but just in case no one has, I hereby do: the episode, which dominates one strand of the plot for quite a long time, begins in chapter 13, where the Valentine is described as follows: "a gorgeously illuminated and embossed design in post-octavo which had been bought on the previous market-day at the chief stationer's in Casterbridge. In the centre was a small oval enclosure; this was left blank, that the sender might insert tender words more appropriate to the special occasion than any generalities by a printer could possibly be."

William W. Morgan
Department of English—4240   Ph: (309) 438-7158—Office
Illinois State University   (309) 452-1204—Home
Normal, IL 61790—4240   E-mail: wwmorgan@rs6000.cmp.ilstu.edu

From   JORDAN@PSYCHOLOGY.NEWCASTLE.EDU.AU
Date: Fri, 4 Aug 1995 10:04:39 GMT+1000
From: Ellen Jordan <JORDAN@PSYCHOLOGY.NEWCASTLE.EDU.AU>
Reply to: VICTORIA 19th-Century British Culture & Society <VICTORIA@IUBVM.UCS.INDIANA.EDU>
To: Multiple recipients of list VICTORIA <VICTORIA@IUBVM.UCS.INDIANA.EDU>
Subject: Re: Valentines in novels

I seem to be making a lot of references lately to Flora Thompson's Lark Rise to Candleford (reminiscences published in the early 1940s of a woman born in 1877 who grew up in an agricultural hamlet in Oxfordshire in the 1880s and worked in the post office of a small town near Buckingham in the 1890s). She also has something to say about valentines in the 1890s that may interest the inquirer: "Another outlet for the few who had venomous minds was the sending of so-called comic valentines addressed in disguised handwriting. The custom of sending daintily printed and bedecked valentines by friends and lovers had by that time died out. Laura was born too late ever to receive a genuine valentine. But what were known as comic valentines were still popular in country districts. These were crude coloured prints on flimsy paper representing hideous forms and faces intended to be more or less appropriate to the recipient. A valentine could be obtained suitable to be sent to one of any trade, calling, or tendency, with words, always insulting and often obscene, calculated to wound, and these, usually unstamped, passed through the village post offices in surprising numbers every Valentine's Eve."
[lines deleted]
(pp. 556 in the 1954 Oxford World's Classics edition.)

Ellen Jordan
Department of Sociology
University of Newcastle,
Australia

Even when people need help with a factual matter and check standard sources, e-mail group participants can often provide additional insight and information, as we can see in the following exchange, also from VICTORIA.

FIGURE 3.14 Question and Answer on VICTORIA

From medevoto@EMAIL.UNC.EDUSun Aug 6 11:15:18 1995
Date: Wed, 2 Aug 1995 09:24:58 -0400
From: Marya Devoto <medevoto@EMAIL.UNC.EDU>
Reply to: VICTORIA 19th-Century British Culture & Society <VICTORIA@IUBVM.UCS.INDIANA.EDU>
To: Multiple recipients of list VICTORIA <VICTORIA@IUBVM.UCS.INDIANA.EDU>
Subject: Gambling

I'm tracking a reference in Mary Shelley's _Rambles_ to Rouge-et-Noir, a casino game that involves, obviously, betting on red or black. A gambling dictionary I consulted and the OED give a 1791 reference and a definition asserting that Rouge-et-Noir is a card game, but the other day
I happened to pick up _Nicholas Nickleby_ only to find a reference to Rouge-et-Noir that mentions, repeatedly, a rolling ball, although it does not mention the bets on numbers that I associate with roulette. Do any rakes among you know when and whether Rouge-et-Noir evolved into roulette, or whether they co-existed, and when a ball might have appeared on the scene?

Thanks for any help you can give.

Marya DeVoto
University of North Carolina
at Chapel Hill
medevoto@email.unc.edu

From robinson@BRAHMS.UDEL.EDUSun Aug 6 11:15:26 1995
Date: Wed, 2 Aug 1995 10:50:35 -0400
From: Charles Robinson <robinson@BRAHMS.UDEL.EDU>
Reply to: VICTORIA 19th-Century British Culture & Society <VICTORIA@IUBVM.UCS.INDIANA.EDU>
To: Multiple recipients of list VICTORIA <VICTORIA@IUBVM.UCS.INDIANA.EDU>
Subject: Re: Gambling

Mary Shelley's knowledge of Rouge et Noir may have been from a book issued by Charles Ollier, P. B. (and Mary) Shelley's publisher, in 1821. Although MWS was in Italy at the time and did not return till 1823, it is possible that she was acquainted with the book through Ollier—Ollier in
1825 went to work for Colburn, then Colburn and Bentley, then Bentley, and had many dealings with MWS over the years. Anyway, the book is as follows:
[Read, Sir William]. _Rouge et Noir in Six Cantos (The Game The Palais Royal Frescati The Salon The Sharper The Guillotine) Versailles and Other Pieces._ London: C And J Ollier Vere Street BNond Street, 1821.
The book was issued on 27 March 1821, a second edtion has a preface dated 9 April, the second edition was advertised 18 May in the Morning Chronicle, and the book was reviewed in Maga in November 1821.

Charles E. Robinson   (302) 831-3654
English Department   robinson@brahms.udel.edu
University of Delaware
Newark DE 19716

E-mail groups are also a great help when a question requires both information and interpretation. For example, there are many questions on the literary groups that ask why a character would do or say a certain thing. These questions sometimes combine a need for factual background on legal, political, or social issues, as well as literary insight. The following messages on Trollope show this:

FIGURE 3-15 Information Quest on Trollope

From shorten@nic.wat.hookup.netThu Aug 17 13:56:47 1995
Date: Fri, 21 Jul 1995 21:44:16 -0400 (EDT)
From: Jay Shorten <shorten@nic.wat.hookup.net>
Reply to: trollope@world.std.com
To: trollope@world.std.com
Subject: Framley Parsonage question

Hello! How delightful to find this group at last.

Perhaps someone can explain to me why on earth Mark Robarts signed that MP's money bill. The only reason I can guess is that he was stupid. And that is why Framley Parsonage is one of my least favourite novels. Am I missing something which I would have understood had I read it in the 1860s? (What was the significance of the "little bills" anyway? Why did it usually cost so much to get them back? Obviously they are not quite like VISA bills.)

Jay Shorten; shorten@nic.wat.hookup.net

FIGURE 3-16 Reply on Trollope

From SENHRO@cardiff.ac.ukThu Aug 17 13:57:28 1995
Date: Wed, 2 Aug 1995 13:58:52 GMT
From: Hugh Osborne <SENHRO@cardiff.ac.uk>
Reply to: trollope@world.std.com
To: trollope@world.std.com
Subject: Re: Framley Parsonage question and the bill of exchange

The bill of exchange, as featured in FP and elsewhere in AT's

fiction, works as follows:

i) It was virtually impossible to obtain either credit or an overdraft facility from the banks; consequently, if post-obits were not an available, i.e. if one couldn't raise cash on the strength of one's future inheritance (be it land, property, money, etc.), then virtually one's only recourse was to the money-lenders, where one would sign a bill of exchange.

ii) The bill of exchange was, in effect, a promissory (sp.?) note, wherein I the impoverished undersigned promise to pay you the unscrupulous money- lender stlg100 (say) on such-and-such a date.

iii) In return, the unscrupulous money-lender advances me money on the strength of the bill, say stlg20, which money is known as a 'discount'.

iv) The bill now having been discounted, I the impoverished undersigned now have to repay you the unscrupulous money-lender stlg120 (original sum + discount) on the date agreed on the bill; in other words, you have made me a loan of twenty quid with interest at a whopping 500%. Nice work if you can get it.

v) Such-and-such a date arrives, and I am still strapped for cash. I go to you and explain that I am unable to repay the stlg120. 'I do wish you would be punctual,' you chide reprovingly, but after much wrangling, you eventually agree to 'renew' the bill; in other words, I make out another bill, for the same amount (stlg100), with a new date for repayment, in order to stave off the evil hour. I now owe you stlg220 (the original bill, the discount, and the renewed bill), still having only received stlg20. Consequently, interest on the loan now stands at 1000%.

vi) Time Passes. I am still penniless. I need readies. PLEASE lend me a tenner. You reluctantly agree. I write out a new bill for, say stlg50, which you discount for stlg5. So on this new bill, I am -again- effectively paying interest of 1000%.

vii) The date for the ORIGINAL (i.e. renewed) bill rolls up, for which I still owe stlg220. Where am I supposed to find that sort of money, when I'm just an impoverished clerk at Somerset House? I am also aware that I will not be able to pay you the later bill (+ discount) of stlg55. On my bended knees, I beg for another renewal. You agree, but with the proviso that, for simplicity's sake, we combine the two existing bills. I now owe you stlg550 ([stlg100 + stlg20 + stlg100 + stlg50 + stlg5] times 2), having received a grand total of stlg25 for the privilege. Interest=2100%. Ad infinitum.

viii) If only I had found a gullible clergyman to accept liability for the amount by countersigning the original bill...

Best Wishes (hope my math is OK)
Hugh Osborne
School of English Communications and Philosophy
UWCC
Cardiff

The above examples were all related to Victorian literature, but the same principles apply in any subject area, whether it's knitting, home-schooling, kayaking, or Russian history. Each e-mail group has a group of people who are deeply interested in a subject, and who are part of an evolving, continuous, discussion of that subject. The group archives, if available, can be a great resource, and if that doesn't turn up the information your patron needs, the groups generally are willing to answer an occasional question posted on behalf of a nonmember.

STUMPERS

Stumpers is one of the most famous, or infamous, of the Internet e-mail groups for librarians. Unlike the other library groups, which are devoted to the discussion of various professional interests, Stumpers is purely practical. Reference librarians (and others) post their toughest questions to Stumpers, and other members of the group will offer assistance. Sometimes this means the answer, with a proper bibliographic citation, but often all others need to provide is a clue, a missing keyword or hint that enables the original poster to find is needed.

The immediate practicality of Stumpers has given it a certain degree of fame among librarians. There are many librarians who have barely explored the rest of the Internet, but who have gotten help with seemingly impossible questions through Stumpers. The fame of Stumpers is also a problem. Currently hovering around the 1,000 member mark, Stumpers is a very high traffic list, with more than fifty messages on an average day. The extremely high traffic is a problem for members of Stumpers, and many people drop off the list because of it.

Despite the problems caused by its high traffic, Stumpers is a fascinating study of the reference process. It's really an extension of what we have all done with difficult reference questions, when we politely excuse ourselves for a minute to the patron, and then run to the staff room or reference office or wherever off-desk librarians can be found, to repeat the question and look for help. Stumpers works the same way, but gives you a much bigger group of helpers.

Sometimes the question gets answered because another reader simply has superior reference skills, and enjoys the chance to show them off. Sometimes it's a matter of someone else having access to better resources. Often, the question is solved by someone who takes a different approach. Observing the many different approaches to the same question is one of the most interesting aspects of STUMPERS.

Very often, however, the person answering the question has a special subject interest in the area of the question. Other times, it's simply that the other person just knows the answer to the question. This may be from previous reference encounters or personal experience. The collective memory of 1,000 reference librarians is a powerful tool.

Stumpers is great for those questions which cannot be answered because there is an error in the question itself. For example, one questioner asked about a short story or poem about AIDS called "The Wrath of Medusa," which was quickly identified as the Joe Pintauro play, "Raft of the Medusa." Another question was posted on behalf of a patron looking for a poem by John P. Marquand, with the first line "You do a circle." This was immediately recognized as a poem by Edwin Markham, with the first line "You drew a circle." Computers are good at making quick searches through huge databases and finding matching records, but people, especially librarians, are good at seeing beyond key words and discerning what the searcher probably really wants.

Stumpers is not without its problems. Because of the high number of messages, outbursts of disagreement over two issues occur: questions that are too easy, and chat beyond the questions and answers. Sometimes questions are asked on Stumpers because it is seen as an easy way to answer the question or for the novelty of it, when the question really could be answered easily with basic reference sources, or the help of a few colleagues. When this issue is raised, however, many members point out the educational value of the group for newer librarians, and resist the idea of limiting the submission of questions in any way.

Though chatting beyond questions and answers is an issue, this is difficult to resist on an active group where many members feel that they know each other. It also reflects the nature of reference librarians, who are the kind of people who love information for its own sake, and usually have almost an unquenchable curiosity about everything. Frequently, the questions on STUMPERS will inspire not only answers, but miscellaneous musings on the topic. Even the answers often suggest new questions.

Some of Stumpers problems are also due to the time it may take to distribute messages to this many members world wide, through every type of network connection. The delay of a few hours on such a high traffic group results in many duplicate answers, as members see the question but haven't seen any answers yet. Sometimes there is even the phenomenon members call the "Jeopardy" effect, as some people see answers or partial answers before they have received the question, and try to discern the question so they can add to the answer.

STUMPERS may inspire smaller e-mail groups for librarians within a library system or certain region. Most of the questions that are answered on STUMPERS could probably be answered on a group with one hundred rather than one thousand members, at a far more manageable level. This would take some of the pressure off STUMPERS itself, leaving it for the really difficult questions.

With all of its problems, STUMPERS has been a powerful teaching tool for the thousands of librarians who have spent some time as members of the group. On STUMPERS, librarians are reminded of some essential facts about reference, such as the fact that many questions have more than one right answer. In addition, it's been one of the great public experiments in global cooperative librarianship, as members from several different countries and many different types of libraries tackle tough ones together.

FINDING THE E-MAIL GROUPS

How do you find an e-mail group dedicated to a particular subject? Like any other reference question, there are many different approaches to this problem. There is no list, on paper or online, that can ever be 100 percent current and complete, but there are a number of places that you can look.

BOOKS

One of the easiest approaches is to do it the old-fashioned way: look in a book. Although new groups are being formed constantly, and others occasionally change locations or disband, most of the larger, more stable groups can be found in any recent Internet directory.

NEW-LIST

One good way to learn about e-mail groups is through New-list. New-list is an e-mail group, also available through USENET as bit.listserv.new-list, which exists for the sole purpose of announcing new e-mail groups. The archives of New-list are also an important source of information about e-mail lists, and can be searched. This is a great, low-traffic group to join, just for the fascination of watching the same technology being used to support such diverse interests. For example, here is the index for one week's New-list digest:

FIGURE 3.17 New-List Announcements

Date: Mon, 21 Aug 1995 00:00:01 -0500
From: Automatic digest processor
             <LISTSERV@VM1.NODAK.EDU>
Reply to: NEW-LIST - New List Announcements <NEW-
             LIST@VM1.NODAK.EDU>
To: Recipients of NEW-LIST digests <NEW-
             LIST@VM1.NODAK.EDU>
Subject: NEW-LIST Digest - 13 Aug 1995 to 20 Aug 1995

There are 21 messages totalling 978 lines in this issue.

Topics of the week:

1. NEW: CELESTINE-L - Discussion of Celestine Prophecy
2. NEW: spouse-support - Bisexual/Straight Spouse Support
3. CHANGE: SCHIZ-L - Schizophrenia Research List (new server address)
4. NEW: IWatch - Internet/Web Site Locator Resource Digest
5. NEW: EH&S Book/Course Catalogue by E-Mail
6. CHANGE: bedrock-list - Bedrock Online - Flintstones Mailing List
7. NEW: WinSock-L-Announce - File uploads to WinSock-L Archive
8. CHANGE: ROOTS-L - Genealogical Research / Genealogy
9. NEW: psa-public-sphere - Psychoanalysis and the Public Sphere
10. NEW: CENTER-L - Centering Prayer Mailing List
11. NEW: SOCRATES - Theoretical and philosophical foundations of psychology
12. NEW: Today - Today In History Mailing List
13. NEW: DB4DOS-L - DataBoss for DOS List
14. NEW: ENVSEC_D - Environment, Population, and Security
15. NEW: DB4WIN-L - DataBoss for Windows
16. NEW: HUDSON-R - Hudson River List
17. NEW: AMKDEV - Apple Media Kit Developers' Discussion List
18. NEW: NFL-List - A general NFL football discussion list
19. NEW: METAB-L - For professionals on Inborn Errors of Metabo-lism
20. NEW: Discuss-Draw - CorelDRAW Discussion List
21. NEW: CUSTOMERNEWS - Corel Customer News mailing list

New-list is an example of a one-way e-mail list, one that exists for sending out announcements rather than for discussion. You can join New-list by sending the usual Listserv subscription message, SUBSCRIBE NEW-LIST [Firstname Lastname] to the following address LISTSERV@vm1.nodak.edu. If you want to receive the list as a digest, wait until you receive your welcome message, and then send the command SET NEW-LIST DIGEST to the Listserv address.

BITNET/INTERNET E-MAIL GROUPS

There are a number of online directories of e-mail groups. The Gopher at Baylor University (gopher.baylor.edu) has a searchable "BITNET/Internet E-mail Groups" database. You can find this by connecting to Baylor's Gopher and looking in the Internet directory, as well as through pointers from other Gophers and Web sites. You can search a single term (for example: dogs) or two or more terms. Multiple terms are considered to be joined by the Boolean operator OR, but you can specify the operator AND if you want.

To search for a list on Russian history, for example, you would search RUSSIA AND HISTORY. If you search on RUSSIAN HISTORY, without specifying the AND, you would get all the lists that have the term Russian and all the lists that have the word history. Of course, as with all keyword searching, you need to choose your words carefully and sometimes try more than one approach. In this example, if I search on RUSSIAN HISTORY or RUSSIA AND HISTORY, I wouldn't find the list RUSHIST because the term "Russian" doesn't happen to appear in the record. The search is performed on the description of the list, not just the name.

Here's the result of the search on RUSSIA AND HISTORY:

FIGURE 3.18 Listing for RUSHIST

List: RUSHIST@VM.USC.EDU
Subscription Address: LISTSERV@VM.USC.EDU
Owner: Valentine Smith <cdell@vax1.umkc.edu>
Last Update: 6/12/92
Description:
 This list is a forum for the reasonable discussion of
 any aspect of the history of Russia from the reign of Ivan III
 (1462-1505) to the end of the Romanov dynasty in the person of
 Nicholas II (1894-1917). Any element of this period is discussable.

DIRECTORY OF SCHOLARLY ELECTRONIC CONFERENCES

One of the best known lists of e-mail groups and other subject-oriented forums is the *Directory of Scholarly Electronic Conferences*. The Directory was created and is maintained by a team at Kent State University headed by Diane Kovacs, and is often called the Kovacs list. The Directory lists electronic conferences, including e-mail groups, USENET newsgroups, and other subject-oriented Internet conferences on scholarly topics.

The Kovacs list is widely available by FTP, Gopher, and the World Wide Web, and you can even have the files sent to you through e-mail. In addition to being a practical resource guide, it is worth examination as a model of Internet publishing. The list is divided into several different subject areas, with editors assigned to each section. The list is well-organized, verified, and updated on a regular basis. There are many pointers to this well-known, valuable resource, and it is also available in print from the Association of Research Libraries. Gopher users can find the list by connecting to the University of Saskatchewan, gopher.usask.edu, choosing "Computing" and then "Internet Information."

World Wide Web users can use the following URL: http://www.mid.net/KOVACS/

The Directory of Scholarly Electronic Conferences is a good example of a grassroots effort to add value to the Internet, by filling a role in filtering, organizing, and presenting information about Internet resources. Diane Kovacs is a librarian whose professional skills lead her and her colleagues to identify a need in the academic community which she then filled with a high quality resource. At this writing, the Directory is in its ninth edition, and it continues to grow. Originally just a list of e-mail groups, the Directory is now including new kinds of forums, such as MUDs and MOOs, which are text-based multi-user environments traditionally used for games, and now experimentally being used for other types of communication. There are many pioneer *infopreneurs* on the Internet, who saw a need and made a modest attempt to fill it, revising and expanding their projects over time.

E-MAIL, STILL THE ONE

The Internet has expanded and evolved dramatically over the past few years, with the development of the World Wide Web, the move to multimedia, and the entrance of commercial interests. Through all this change, one thing has remained unchanged on the Internet, and that is e-mail. For many people, having e-mail is what defines being on the Internet, and while they may explore other resources, e-mail for many people is their home base.

When most people have a question about something, their natural inclination is not to visit the library or do independent research; it is to ask a friend, neighbor, family member, or teacher for information, advice, or ideas. E-mail groups are just an electronic extension of this natural form of information-seeking behavior. By tapping into these groups, librarians can be a part of this process, and can get answers to questions and strengthen collections to help improve service to our own patrons.

4 USENET NEWSGROUPS

USENET is the world's largest bulletin board system, a huge cooperative worldwide exchange of messages on thousands of different subjects. USENET is not a network in the sense of being a group of computers that are connected to each other, but rather it is a cooperative network of various types of systems which receive and pass along the flow of messages posted on the various USENET newsgroups.

WHAT IS USENET?

USENET is now intimately tied to the Internet, but it was not always so, and to comprehend the complexity and nature of USENET, it is helpful to first understand USENET's history. USENET began in 1979 as an exchange of messages between two neighboring colleges, the University of North Carolina and Duke University. They used the UNIX utility, Unix to Unix Copy Program (UUCP), to pass messages from system to system over phone lines. USENET, or Unix Users Network, fit right in with the UNIX culture, which is essentially a community of programmers who use the UNIX toolkit to create new shared UNIX tools. The original USENET institutions were not part of the ARPANET and the use of UUCP to pass formatted messages back and forth and display them in an organized fashion to users on each system was an interesting use of basic UNIX tools. Information about USENET was distributed at the USENIX (UNIX Users) conference in 1980, and other institutions soon joined the original two institutions. As networks became part of the evolving Internet, the Internet became the major route of passage for USENET traffic. However, there are still sites that are part of USENET but not Internet, as well as sites that are on the Internet but not USENET. USENET is sometimes described as a highly organized system and sometimes as an anarchy, and both descriptions have some truth. USENET is organized because most Systems Administrators take their responsibilities seriously, depend on each other's cooperation to serve their own site's needs, and adhere to certain generally accepted USENET conventions. USENET is an anarchy in the sense that it is completely decentralized and without authority, and there is no central site to apply sanctions or prohibit any type of activity.

USENET is such an important part of the Internet world that some people use the terms Internet and USENET interchangeably. For example, they might say "Here's a story I heard on the Internet . . . " or "I found a great guacamole recipe on the Internet." It would be more accurate to say they found these things on USENET. Think of USENET in terms of content, and the Internet in terms of means of transmission. USENET is the collective flow of organized messages and the cooperative arrangements among systems that keep the messages flowing.

The Internet provides a fast and reliable way for USENET messages to travel, but there are many smaller sites that participate in USENET by other means. For example, smaller BBS systems may receive USENET by UUCP, the Unix-to-Unix Copy Program. A telephone connection with another system is established on some regular basis, allowing new USENET messages to be downloaded to the BBS and outgoing messages to be uploaded to the other system. UUCP, and not the Internet, was the original method of USENET transmission, and is still in use.

It is also possible to have full Internet access without having access to USENET. Full Internet access generally means having a system that is connected by a router to another system on the Internet, using TCP/IP for the three basic Internet protocols: e-mail, telnet, and FTP. These three protocols serve as the building blocks for much other activity, such as Gopher and the World Wide Web. In order to participate in USENET, a system on the Internet has to take an additional step and make arrangements with another USENET site to receive a complete or partial USENET feed. This means designating a Systems Administrator to manage the USENET activity, setting aside a certain amount of disk space for the messages, setting up local software to administer the USENET messages (performing such tasks as purging messages that have been on the system for some specified amount of time) and administering client software for reading and posting to the USENET newsgroups.

This is an area where librarians are somewhat out of step with users. Almost all of our patrons who have Internet access at home use commercial Internet service providers who generally provide USENET access, or through college systems which also usually are part of USENET, and libraries whose Internet access is limited to a dial-in account on another system usually have access to USENET on that other system. However, when libraries connect their own library systems on the Internet, they are far less apt to have USENET, since many library systems have not been able to invest the local time and resources in setting up USENET access on their own system.

Even if librarians do not have direct USENET access on their own systems, however, they should become familiar with USENET and how it works for a couple of reasons. The first is that so many of our patrons have USENET access; if we want them to perceive us as having any understanding of the Internet at all, we should be familiar with USENET and be able to provide information about it. The other is that USENET's influence is ubiquitous on the Internet. Many of the USENET newsgroups have created various files and projects that can be found on Gopher and the World Wide Web. The USENET groups have been the leading force in organizing and creating content that is made freely available over the Internet.

USENET's original purpose was to serve as a bulletin board in the most traditional sense, a place for the posting of announcements, and that heritage lives on in the terminology of USENET. We refer to USENET as "the news" and use terms such as articles, newsreaders, and newsgroups. Despite the journalistic terminology, USENET is primarily a forum for conversation rather than news.

USENET HIERARCHIES

USENET news is organized into different hierarchies, each representing a different broad subject area. Within each hierarchy, there are many different newsgroups, representing different discussion topics. Within the *soc* or social groups, for example, there are a number of *culture* groups, with names like soc.culture.italy and soc.culture.african-american. In addition to soc, there is *rec* for recreation, *sci* for science, *comp* for computers, *talk* for conversation, *misc* for miscellaneous, and *news* for talk about USENET itself. These are the original or mainstream hierarchies, sometimes referred to as the Big Seven, carried by almost all USENET sites. The Big Seven has recently become the Big Eight, with the addition of *humanities*.

In addition, there are many other hierarchies which have been created for special purposes. For example, *k12* is for the discussion of education. *Biz* is for business-oriented discussions, and explicitly allows advertising, considered a violation of netiquette on the mainstream groups. *Gnu* is for discussion of the Free Software Foundation's GNU project. *Bit.listserv* is a gateway for the BITNET's Listserv e-mail groups, allowing those who prefer to read and participate through USENET rather than e-mail.

There are also many regional hierarchies for different parts of the country (for example, *ne* for New England) or different countries (for example, *de* for Germany.) The regional hierarchies usually have several different newsgroups, with names like ne.weather, ne.jobs, ne.housing, etc., and one group for miscellaneous postings, called ne.general.

One important special hierarchy is *clari*, short for Clarinet. This is a private commercial service that distributes news and features using USENET protocols. If your system has subscribed to this service, you will have access to groups with names like clari.news.bulletin for major breaking stories, clari.local.massachusetts and similar groups for every state, clari.biz.market.ny for New York Stock Exchange reports, and clari.sports.baseball for baseball news and scores. The Clarinet news comes from a variety of reputable sources, including a live UPI newswire. In addition to the news, Clarinet carries many popular features, including columnists like Dave Barry and Miss Manners. Although Clarinet uses the format of USENET news, clari groups are one-way distribution lists and readers may not post to them.

Alt or Alternative, is a much discussed and frequently misunderstood hierarchy. Alt has a number of strange and bizarre groups, as well a number of sexually explicit groups. There are alt groups where rudeness and flaming are not only tolerated, but expected. In fact, there is actually a groups called alt.flame. However, what is really alternative about the alt groups is not the content, but the method of establishment. The process of starting a group in one of the mainstream hierarchies is tightly controlled, requiring proposals, discussion, and formal votes by USENET systems administrators. Alt groups tend to be formed more casually. In fact, juvenile techies often figure out how to set up bogus newsgroups for the questionable thrill of seeing group names like alt.flame.barney.die.die.die.

TECHNICAL DETAILS

When a system becomes a USENET site, the System Administrator installs news management and newsreader software on the local system, and arranges to receive a newsfeed from another system. The feed probably includes the mainstream hierarchies, and some of the alternative and local hierarchies. This may not include every group within a particular hierarchy.

Users read and post to USENET through newsreader software.

If you are using a terminal on a mainframe system or dialing in to a shell account on a commercial system, your newsreader program will be on the host system and you will be limited to the newsreader software chosen by the Systems Administrator, typically one or more UNIX-based programs such as rn, trn, or tin. If you have a direct connection or are dialing in to a SLIP/PPP account, you will want to choose your own PC or Macintosh program. In addition to special newsreader software, you may be reading and posting to USENET through an e-mail program such as Pine, or a World Wide Web client such as Netscape.

The choice of newsreader software is important and will influence your opinion of USENET. Some programs work well for people who want to belong to a few groups and read them thoroughly, and others are better for people who want to scan lots of groups and only read messages with subject lines of particular interest. If you have a choice, try a few different readers and see which one fits your personal style. Librarians who are using the newsgroups for reference rather than their own personal interests may prefer a newsgroup like tin which allows you to quickly scan many groups looking at the subjects in each. You can subscribe to the groups most useful for reference at your library, and scan them when you have a relevant question, posting as needed.

When you begin to read USENET, your system will set up a file in your directory called *.newsrc* to keep track of your subscriptions. With USENET, subscribing is purely local, a matter of telling the newsreader program to display a particular group for you and to keep track of the messages you've read. Within each group, there are individual postings or messages, which are identified by number. A message posted to soc.culture.italy, for example, might be given the number soc.culture.italy.5308.

Once you have a message, you can use your newsreader software to post a response. The next time your system communicates with its USENET provider, it will pick up your message and pass it along to other sites. You can also decide to respond via e-mail to someone directly, rather than posting a general reply to the whole newsgroup. Newsreader software also generally allows you to set distribution options, so that your postings may only be distributed to systems in a particular area or country rather than to the whole world.

LIFE ON USENET

The following shows a Group Selection screen in my favorite newsreader, tin. The format is a numbered list, with the names of each group and a description, if one has been set up by the group's administrator. The number in the second column is the number of unread messages in each group. Messages are kept on a system for a certain length of time, typically two weeks to a month, and then are deleted from the system, so these numbers fluctuate even if you never read any messages, as new messages are received and older ones are deleted.

FIGURE 4.1 Tin: Group Selection Screen

Group Selection (42)   h=help

1		soc.libraries.talk	Discussing all aspects of libraries
2	732	rec.answers	Repository for periodic USENET art
3	1776	rec.arts.books	Books of all genres, and the publi
4	285	alt.psychology.help	An alt.support group away from hom
5	734	alt.support.attn-deficit	Attention Deficit Disorder.
6	2568	rec.org.mensa	Talking with members of the high I
7	782	ne.general	General interest discussions perti
8	2825	alt.comedy.british	Discussion of British comedy in a
9		rec.arts.tv	The boob tube, its history, and pa
10	154	alt.fan.rumpole	
11	379	rec.arts.movies	Discussions of movies and movie ma
12	3427	news.groups	
13	1021	rec.food.veg	Vegetarians.
14	1977	news.answers	
15	421	alt.quotations	Quotations, quips, .sig lines, wit
16	429	alt.fan.cecil-adams	The brother Douglas Adams never ta

<n>=set current to n, TAB=next unread, /=search pattern, c)atchup,
g)oto, j=line down, k=line up, h)elp, m)ove, q)uit, r=toggle all/unread,
s)ubscribe, S)ub pattern, u)nsubscribe, U)nsub pattern, y)ank in/out

---

Once a group is selected to read, you get the Thread Selection screen. The term *thread* means a group of messages on the same topic. The term is used in both e-mail groups and USENET, but the definition on USENET is more specific. News posting software allows for the posting of follow-up messages, which not only take their subject line from the original message, but are linked for display purposes if a threaded newsreader such as trn or tin is used.

FIGURE 4.2 Tin: Thread Selection Screen

alt.quotations (181T 421A 0K 0H R)   h=help

1 + 2	Quotes on Perseverance	Kimberly Hullfish
2 + 2	Two friends in love	casioc@orplid.shne
3 + 5	looking for John Lennon quotes	Richard Wallaert
4 + 2	Service	Barry Fetter
5 + 2	Warhol Quote	Richard J. Sagall,
6 + 3	Books	Michael McMullin
7 + 3	REQ: Verbal excesses, jargon, diplomacy etc.	Tom
8 + 2	>>> Need a Date?? <<< Call Now! 1-900-267	Bill Clinton
9 +	Einstein Quotations v.2	Erik Max Francis
10 + 5	Maharishi qoute: no problems	Ren Hoek
11 +	Personal quote from a friend	Darren Chng
12 +	Source Req. "Nature who washed her hands	Chalon Parker
13 + 6	turret gunner	Mr. Pink
14 +	An unexamined life...	Charles Deremer
15 +	Request for quotes on THE SEA	Håvard Fosseng
16 + 4	REQ: Quotes about learning	Håvard Fosseng

<n>=set current to n, TAB=next unread, /=search pattern, ^K)ill/select,
a)uthor search, c)atchup, j=line down, k=line up, K=mark read, l)ist thread,
|=pipe, m)ail, o=print, q)uit, r=toggle all/unread, s)ave, t)ag, w=post

---

In this case, we see sixteen different threads or ongoing discussions in the group alt.quotations. In each case we see the subject line from the original message and, to the left, the number of follow-up messages. For example, there is a message called "Quotes on perseverance" plus two follow-up messages.

In this thread selection screen, we also see evidence of something that has become common on USENET, an irrelevant, unsolicited message, generally posted to advertise a product or service, promote a chain letter, or some otherwise inappropriate activity. In this case we have the "Get a Date" message advertising a 900 line. As is often the case, the sender has concealed his or her true identity, hiding behind the obviously forged "Bill Clinton."

This message is an example of spamming, the practice of having an automated program send hundreds of copies of a message to different groups, regardless of the subject. The term was inspired by the classic Monty Python "spam spam spam spam" sketch. Spamming is universally condemned on USENET as a violation of netiquette, but still persists.

Moving beyond the Thread Selection screen, you can read the messages that have been posted to the group. For example, here is a response to a question on the source of a quotation. The person quoted part of the original message, which his software put into the response and set off with the ">" [greater-than] symbol. Quoting a few lines from the original message can be useful, especially for people who may be reading messages out of order using a non-threaded newsreader. However, it is considered very annoying to quote the entire previous message in a response.

FIGURE 4.3 Quoted Message and Response

```
Sat, 09 Sep 1995 20:21:21      alt.quotations        Thread  70 of 180
Lines 19              Re: Sleep of Reason?      Respno  1 of  3
shapiro@minerva.cis.yale.edu              Fred Shapiro at Yale University


On 9 Sep 1995, Mike Finley wrote:

> Sages and know-wells — who said:
>
> "The sleep of reason breeds monsters?"

Francisco Jose de Goya y Lucientes.  In plate 43 of _Los Caprichos_
(1799), the artist rests, his head in his arms, on a desk inscribed with
this line (in Spanish, "el sueno de la razon produce monstruos").  Behind
him hover monstrous owls, bats, and a great cat.  (Doesn't anyone on this
newsgroup have Bartlett's Quotations?)

++++++++++++++++++++++++++++++++++++++++++++++++++++++++++++++++++++++++++
+++
+ Fred R. Shapiro                        Editor                       +
+ Associate Librarian for Public Services   OXFORD DICTIONARY OF
AMERICAN  +
+ Yale Law School                        LEGAL QUOTATIONS       +
+ e-mail: shapiro@minerva.cis.yale.edu   (Oxford University Press)
++++++++++++++++++++++++++++++++++++++++++++++++++++++++++++++++++++++++++
+++
```

LIBRARIANS ON USENET

Librarians have tended to be more involved with e-mail groups rather than USENET. With the exception of the Listserv groups that are also available in USENET in the Bit.listserv hierarchy, there is only one library-related e-mail group, soc.libraries.talk. However, USENET has many benefits for librarians. The fact that subscribing on USENET is purely local makes it easy for librarians to drop in on a group, read recent postings, and post a question on behalf of a patron, later just unsubscribing from the group.

In fact, some librarians might want to subscribe to a number of high interest newsgroups, checking them only occasionally or when they have a question to post. This would not be a good idea with e-mail groups, where subscriptions can quickly fill up your mailbox, demanding your attention.

Librarians can post messages to USENET groups looking for specific information on behalf of a patron. You can also post messages to USENET looking for ideas for collection development, booklists, displays, or programs. First, you should be sure that you are familiar with any booklists the group maintains, which we will be discussing later in the book. But if a group doesn't have such a list, or you want recommendations on a particular aspect of a subject or for new books, feel free to ask. Most people are pleased to be asked to recommend books to librarians, and will often go out of their way to carefully choose certain books and explain their choices.

Librarians who participate in USENET should also look for opportunities to use their special skills at organizing and presenting information. If you request recommendations for vegetarian cookbooks or Civil War biographies, organize the responses you receive into a booklist, and post it to the group. If you see questions posted that you can easily answer from basic reference sources, take a few minutes to do so. You will also find many opportunities when you can recommend books to people, or to refer them to their own libraries for help. Librarians should be contributors of information and not just consumers; it's good netiquette and good public relations as well.

Librarians can get questions on almost any topic, which is why we can appreciate the infinite variety of USENET. There are groups devoted to roller coasters, chess, bird watching, and politics, as well as various aspects of science, education, computers, and much more. USENET allows librarians to drop in on any group and post a message when they are trying to track down some information on behalf of a patron.

There are certain groups, however, that are especially useful to librarians, and that deserve some special attention.

ALT.QUOTATIONS

Alt.quotations is a great resource for tracking down the source of a quotation, or for gathering quotations on a particular theme. It is an interesting group to watch, just to see how frequently quotations are misquoted and misattributed, even in published sources. Many quotations become associated, at least in the public mind, with people who have quoted the original lines. Sometimes a quotation question will go back through several layers of attribution before getting to the presumably original speaker.

It is also interesting to see how frequently the same few quotations come up for discussion, over and over. "When they came for the Jews . . ." is often discussed on alt.quotations. This is a difficult one, since the phrase was used by Martin Niemoller in a number of different versions in speeches, and does not appear in his writings. "Desiderata," the poem that begins "Go placidly amid the noise and haste . . ." has a long and complicated history of misattribution. It was written by Max Ehrman in 1927, and in 1956 was distributed by St. Paul's Church in Baltimore to its members It was then copied from the church publication and widely redistributed with the erroneous note that it was found in Old St. Paul's Church dated 1692, the date the church was founded. This error persists to this day despite frequent attempts to correct the record. But possibly the most common quotation asked on alt.quotations is Hillel's "If not now, when?" which has been attributed to various people including Golda Meir and Martin Luther King.

In addition to people seeking the source or correct wording of a quotation, the group is also used for gathering favorite quotations on a certain subject or theme, for example, education, patience, or health.

ALT.FAN.CECIL-ADAMS

Alt.fan.cecil-adams is a free-wheeling, open forum on a variety of questions. It is related to Cecil Adams' newspaper column and books called "The Straight Dope." Most of the questions here are not formal reference questions, just the questions that curious people have as they try to make sense of the world. The discussions on this group follow the irreverent, funny, sometimes sarcastic style of "The Straight Dope," and the conversation is often quite uninhibited. However, lots of potentially useful information for reference librarians comes through this group, as well as an opportunity for the type of rambling discussions that can be such a problem on Stumpers.

REC.ARTS.MOVIES

Another useful group is rec.arts.movies, which discusses every aspect of movies, old and new. This is a good place to post a question when your patron is trying to identify a movie but can't remember anything useful in terms of key word searching, just various aspects of the plot. It's also good if you have a patron who is looking for movies which illustrate a certain theme or depict some event.

REC.MUSIC

The music groups such as rec.music.classical are helpful when you have a patron who is trying to identify a piece of music used in a movie or television commercial. The groups are also good for roundup-type questions. For example, a recent question asked which composers had tinnitus. There are specialized music groups on a wide variety of styles and types of music, as well as individual groups and performers.

SOC.CULTURE

The soc.culture groups, such as soc.culture.france, are a great source of information when you have a patron who is planning a trip or studying a certain area or culture. They are also a great help when a patron is trying to understand some cultural difference between two societies, the meaning of some phrase or expression, or trying to track down an allusion in a book or movie. Often these are allusions to food; for example, the Australians and New Zealanders frequently have to explain what Pavlova is.

COLLECTING

There are groups dedicated to collectors of everything from old books to eight-track tapes, and these can be useful if a patron is trying to identify something found in the attic or purchased at a flea market. Of course, nobody can give appraisals without seeing a certain object, but USENET groups can give general guidelines and helpful pointers for more information.

LOCAL AND REGIONAL GROUPS

If you have access to local or regional groups, they can be very useful. For example, in my own area we have a hierarchy called ne, for New England. Ne.weather is great for tracking down information on famous storms, hurricanes, blizzards, and tornados in the area, often used by local journalists who are writing "You think *this* storm was bad . . . " articles. Ne.general is great for questions about local sources for various kinds of ethnic food, shoe stores specializing in hard to find sizes, and various other topics purely of local interest.

PETS GROUPS

There are also a number of very active groups on different types of pets. Rec.pets.dogs and rec.pets.cats are especially active. The pet groups are excellent at collecting and maintaining Frequently Asked Question files, which tends to raise the quality of the general group traffic.

COOKING GROUPS

Another group that's potentially helpful for public library reference is rec.food.cooking. If you have a patron who is looking for a particular recipe remembered from a magazine, newspaper column, or old cookbook, the rec.food.cooking people can probably help. There are also specialized groups such as rec.food.historic and rec.food.veg for vegetarian issues.

NETIQUETTE ON USENET

Beyond the general principles of Netiquette that apply to both e-mail and USENET, there are a few special reminders that apply to USENET.

CROSS-POSTING

Cross-posting is the practice of sending the same message to more than one newsgroup. There are times when this is appropriate, for example, the question on composers with tinnitus might have been posted to both rec.music.classical and alt.support.tinnitus. However, cross-posting can quickly get out of hand, and cause a lot of confusion when follow-ups from one group continue to be cross-posted to both. Use this facility sparingly, if at all, and be sure to look at the headers when posting follow-ups to remove irrelevant groups.

TEST MESSAGES

Sometimes you want to send a test message to see if your newsposting software is working and to make sure that you understand how to use it. There are special test groups, such as alt.test, that exist for this purpose. Never post messages to other groups with the subject line "Testing" or "Please ignore." This is very annoying to people who are scanning through the chaff, looking for the wheat.

QUOTING

When you are posting a follow-up message, you shouldn't quote the entire original message, even if your software does that automatically. Most people will be reading your message through a threaded newsreader, and will have just read the original message. The best thing you can do is paraphrase the original message so that anyone will understand your message, even if he or she hasn't read the original. For example, instead of saying, "Try Clyde Edgerton or Kaye Gibbons!" you should write, "In answer to the request for modern Southern authors to include in a book discussion group, I would suggest Clyde Edgerton and Kaye Gibbons." If necessary, you can quote a few lines of the original message for clarity.

HOMEWORK AND TERM PAPER QUESTIONS

There are many students with access to USENET, and they sometimes try to use the groups as a shortcut for homework assignments or writing term papers. For example, they post messages to rec.arts.books that say, "Compare and contrast the treatment of women in Victorian England as portrayed by Charles Dickens and in Industrial America as portrayed by Upton Sinclair."

Although USENET readers are generally always willing to discuss any topic, they do draw the line at such blatant laziness. They will, however, enter into a discussion on various points of a topic like this with a student whose project is well under way.

Librarians would never indulge in such behavior, but as information professionals, we should hold ourselves to a higher standard when it comes to doing our homework before posting to USENET. Don't post a question to alt.quotations if the answer is in Bartlett's, and when you do post a question, explain what sources you have already consulted.

REPLIES BY E-MAIL

If you post a question to USENET, you may get responses by e-mail or posted to the group, but it is considered rude to request responses by e-mail. Many people believe that if the question is posted to the group and seen by all, the answer should be there as well, and that people who can't take the trouble to look for their answers shouldn't be posting questions.

GETTING USENET ACCESS

What can you do if your system is on the Internet, but doesn't offer the USENET newsgroups? The first thing you should do is talk to your Systems Administrator to see if such access is planned, and to indicate your interest.

If your own system doesn't have access, there are a few alternatives you can explore. There are some gateway services that make USENET news available from Gopher or the World Wide

Web. One such service is Mercury at Michigan State University (gopher.msu.edu). You can find others by connecting to any large Gopher and looking for a menu item called Internet Gateways, USENET news, or a similar heading. However, such gateways are generally overused and slow. Also, a public system can't manage subscriptions for you and keep track of what you have already read, making this the worst way to try to read the news.

A better alternative is to get an account on another system which does offer USENET. You might find a public system that will allow you to set up an account and read the news for free, although these are becoming rare, or you might choose a commercial service and set up an account. If you continue to use your primary system for e-mail and other Internet services, and only connect to the commercial service for USENET, this should be very inexpensive. You can telnet from your home system to the commercial system, eliminating phone charges. This is well worth considering, at least on a trial basis.

There is also a fascinating, free service offered by Stanford University, called HotPage, the Stanford Netnews Filtering Service. You send an e-mail message with the command "subscribe," a word or phrase that you want them to search, and a period (from 1-5) that corresponds to how often (in days) you want to receive messages. For example, I might send the following message:

FIGURE 4.4 Subscription Message for HotPage

To: netnews@hotpage.stanford.edu
Subject:
subscribe Cape Cod
period 5

The service searches through all incoming USENET messages, and every five days will send me an e-mail message with the message headers and first several lines of any messages that contain the words CAPE COD. If I want to retrieve the complete message, I can send the command "get" and the message ID number. The example here is a simple one, but the service also supports more complex searching. For more information, send the message HELP FAQ to the following address: netnews@hotpage. stanford.edu.

HotPage is a great service but should also serve as a reminder of how very public USENET is. If someone wanted to monitor all your USENET postings, they could do so by setting up a subscription using your name as the search terms. USENET and e-mail groups sometimes feel like private clubs, and there is a feeling of anonymity that sometimes causes people to reveal a great deal about themselves. However, it is important to remember that this is all very public, and messages can be forwarded and saved and archived and indexed in many ways, and old messages can come back to haunt you. You should consider all USENET activity to be public, not private.

IN SEARCH OF INFORMATION

USENET gives you a chance to study the interests, questions, and problems of a vast array of people, from the comfort of your own desk. Many people are on USENET doing something that we can understand: seeking information. But the information-seeking behavior of the average person is quite different from that of the average librarian, and even the average library patron. Most people seek information not by consulting books or databases, but by asking other people: family, friends, colleagues, and, thanks to USENET, total strangers who may be thousands of miles away.

USENET can provide you with instant access to people who know about and care about almost any topic you can imagine. If you are doing reference, you can get answers to impossible questions, with the help of experts and amateurs with a lot of interest and experience in a certain subject area. For collection development, we can use the groups to see which books are considered best in any area by people who really care about the subject. USENET can be a complicated, confusing, and rude world, but it works, and our patrons can benefit if we learn how to use it on their behalf.

5 MEET THE RABBERATTI: REC.ARTS.BOOKS

The largest general forum for all kinds of book-related talk is the USENET newsgroup rec.arts.books. This is a very active group, with dozens of threads active at any given time. The regulars call this group r.a.b. and refer to themselves as the Rabberatti, and are always willing to discuss anything to do with book, authors, bookstores, and the reading life in general. For librarians, it's a fascinating way to observe a group of avid readers, and hear what they think about books, authors, reading, bookstores, and sometimes even libraries.

The first thing that may strike the observer of r.a.b. is how very avid some of these readers are. Many people who post here seem to read several books a week, and the on-going forum of r.a.b. is an important part of their reading lives. Readers often have a great need to discuss what they are reading, but this can be difficult in "real" life. You may have a need to share your thoughts on a certain book or author, but unless you have friends who share the same interests or you read primarily bestsellers, it can be difficult to find anyone interested in discussing what you've just read. Librarians usually have many book-loving colleagues around for lunch hour literary conversations, but others may not be so fortunate.

REC.ARTS.BOOKS: SOMETHING FOR EVERY READER

With rec.arts.books, however, you can almost always find someone willing to discuss almost any book. Many threads begin with someone posting a message that says something like "I just read Anne Tyler's new book and thought it was great, her best ever. What does everyone else think?" Other messages are more specific, asking why a certain character would ever have married that awful man, or killed that lovely woman, or whatever. The deep personal interest in the lives of certain characters and the intensity of the discussion is a great tribute to the power of both the written word and computer networked communications.

Here is a typical screen of messages on rec.arts.books:

FIGURE 5.1 Message Selection Screen on rec.arts.books

```
rec.arts.books (28T 45A 0K 0H R)                          h=help

1  +       Penguin 60s                              Donald A. Hosek
2  + 2     movies improving books                   Gary Lee Stonum
3  + 6     Post Modernism (huh?)                    Silke-Maria Weine
4  + 4     wurst movie corruptions of books         Jim Hartley
5  +       Why print the title on every page?       Michael Richard
6  + 2     Does AI make philosophy obsolete?        Chris"Big-Kahuna"R
7  +       Confederacy of Dunces - film ID?         Judy Wilson
8          What's a Felisberto?                     Robert Schechter
9  +       Books that stock British books           Penguin
10 +       Under the Volcano - I don't get it       lfjed@nmsua.nmsu.e
11 +       Rainer Maria Rilke                       Robert Teeter
12 +       Netochka Nezvanova Question.             Joel Coughlin
13 +       Into a ball (was Re: worst movie corrupti) Dorothy J Heydt
14 +       Maugham kills me!                        Koen Engelborghs
15 + 3     Onomatopoeia                             Miriam
16 + 2     WTB: Modern Library hardbacks w/dust jackets Scot Kamins

<n>=set current to n, TAB=next unread, /=search pattern, ^K)ill/select,
a)uthor search, c)atchup, j=line down, k=line up, K=mark read, l)ist thread,
|=pipe, m)ail, o=print, q)uit, r=toggle all/unread, s)ave, t)ag, w=post
```

COMMON TOPICS ON REC.ARTS.BOOKS

Librarians can learn much about the interests of readers from seeing which topics come up over and over again:

What did you think of . . . [particular book]?

This is probably the most common type of thread on r.a.b. Someone reads a book, and wants to share her opinion. These threads can provoke a lot of disagreement, and occasionally personal stories are exchanged to explain attitudes. For example, someone might say that the mother in the story was just like her own mother, so she could understand how the daughter felt.

What do you think of . . . [particular author]?

This is a variation on the above, and questions about a particular book often turn into a general discussion on an author. The books and authors discussed cover the complete spectrum of time and genre. At any given time, there are apt to be as many people discussing Jane Austen as Stephen King. Victorian authors seem to be particularly popular, as is science fiction, but just about all types of literature is discussed here.

What are the last five books you read?

This is one of the questions that has become a standard, on-going part of rec.arts.books. Books mentioned here often start discussions that break off in separate threads. The first of January always brings lists of favorite books read in the past year and some amazing exchanges of statistics of prolific reading.

Books that changed your life

This is another perennial topic, and a fascinating one for librarians, who share an abiding interest in how reading can affect people. The works cited as having changed someone's life include philosophical, ethical, or psychological works, such as *Man's Search for Meaning* by Viktor Frankl; biographies and autobiographies, such as *The Diary of a Young Girl* by Anne Frank; or fiction of a wide variety. People most often select a book that was read in high school or college, the prime years for forming a sense of personal identity.

Often, however, a person mentions a children's book which he or she feels changed his or her life in one significant way: it made him or her a reader. Some of these messages describe someone, after having a struggle with reading, as becoming inspired to persevere in his or her efforts due to a particular book. Others learned to read easily but needed a special book to show them the power of reading to transport the mind. Almost always, the book was one that they found or that was read to them in the first, second, or third grade. Books mentioned include *The Wind in the Willows, Winnie the Pooh*, and various other classics. Beverly Cleary has been mentioned for her ability to write books that seem real and immediate to children, and reveal children's thoughts and feelings. However, sometimes the books are specifically described as not having any unique literary value, but just having been the right book at the right time.

Bookstores: superstores vs. independents

This has been a constant topic for the past few years. Bookstores in general are discussed far more often than libraries, and people have strong opinions on what they like and dislike. The rise of the chains of superstores like Borders and Barnes and Noble is one of the greatest on-going, vehement areas of disagreement. While some readers love the large selection, convenience, and cappuccino of the giants, others worry about the loss of the independent bookstores and the concentrated power of the chain stores. This topic has been argued from economic, political, social, practical, and ethical viewpoints, along with a lot of sharing of personal experiences at both types of stores from both customers and staff.

Humorous books

If the activity on rec.arts.books is any indicator, there is a great need for laughter in the world. Over and over, people request humorous books. The wording of the initial request almost always includes the phrase "laugh out loud." Responses to this always include P.G. Wodehouse, Mark Twain, E.F. Benson, Tom Sharpe, Kingsley Amis, and J.P. Donleavy, among others, but if r.a.b. is any indication, the funniest book of all time must be "Three Men and a Boat (not to mention the dog)" by Jerome K. Jerome.

Here is a typical message from a "funniest book" thread. This one is a triple-decker, a response to a response to a response, with all or part of the two earlier messages quoted into the third.

FIGURE 5.2 "Funniest Book" Thread on rec.arts.books

Xref: world rec.arts.books:144648
Path:world!news.kei.com!newshost.marcam.com!usc!howland.reston.ans.net!newsfeed.
internetmci.com!tank.news.pipex.net!pipex!in1. uu.net!news.sprintlink.net!earth.superlink.net!usenet
From: pauli@superlink.net (paul ilechko)
Newsgroups: rec.arts.books
Subject: Re: lucky jim—funniest novel written
Date: Sun, 17 Sep 1995 18:49:55 GMT
Organization: SuperNet Inc. (908) 828-8988
Lines: 42
Message-ID: <43hri2$rcq@earth.superlink.net>
References: <43ej5b$tgg@core.bard.edu> <quentin-1609952032580001@line0d.gunn-du.pavilion.co.uk>
NNTP-Posting-Host: p3.superlink.net
X-Newsreader: Forte Free Agent 1.0.82

quentin@pavilion.co.uk (Quentin) wrote:

>In article <43ej5b$tgg@core.bard.edu>, rg587@bard.edu (Ross Goodman) wrote:

>> what book is funnier??
>>
>> r.

>'The Liar', by Stephen Fry,
>Almost everything by PG Wodehouse,
>Saki's short stories,
>Jasoslav Hasek's 'The Good Soldier Svejk'

i have to object - this was one of the worst books i ever failed to
finish reading - even duller than Don Quixote (i'm waiting for the
hate mail ...)

>'The Fall and Rise of Reginal Perrin' by David Nobbs (incidentally, much
>darker and deeper than the TV version),
>'My Family and Other Animals' by Gerald Durrell
>Most of Evelyn Waugh's earlier novels,
> 'Experiences of an Irish RM' by Somerville and Ross
>'Stalky and Co' by Rudyard Kipling,
>Almost anything by Spike Milligan, and, although I hate to mention the two
>in the same sentence, (apologies, Spike, if you read this), most of
>Jeffrey Archer's books - although I believe this may be unintentional.
>TTFN
>Q

additional nominations ..

catch 22 - heller
a frolic of his own - gaddis
jr - gaddis
the roaches have no king - daniel weiss
our man in havana - greene
money - martin amis

    paul

Southern literature

There seems to be a very large group of readers who are interested in reading novels by Southern authors. Often the initial message is something like, "I love Clyde Edgerton [Pat Conroy, Jill McCorkle, Lee Smith . . .] and am looking for other books about the south." This always begins a long thread of responses, listing many favorite authors, sometimes reinforced with personal experiences, such as "I was raised in Kentucky and it was just the way this author describes it!"

Other Subjects or Themes

In addition to requests for humorous books and Southern literature, there are people looking for books with various other themes or characteristics. Very often this is because reading the works of one author awakens a desire to read similar books. Someone who enjoys Patrick O'Brian will look for other nautical fiction, or someone who admires Willa Cather or Margaret Laurence will look for other books set on the prairie. Some readers have looked for books that reflect the experiences of immigrants from different times and places, novels about small town life, and coming-of-age stories. Some are more specific, like the recent request for suggestions for "hard-boiled inner-city crime novels set in the UK."

Other frequent requests are for recommendations for books by and about African-Americans, Asian-Americans, Latinos, and Native Americans. These requests will usually get many responses. There are also frequent requests for fiction involving scientists, engineers, architects, librarians, or other professional groups, which also generate a lot of interest. These discussions are a great source of ideas for booklists, displays, book discussion groups, etc.

Here's a thread of this type from the Historical Fiction group, another triple-decker:

FIGURE 5.3 Looking for Fiction Set in Ancient Rome

Xref: world rec.arts.books.hist-fiction:1838
Path:world!news.kei.com!simtel!news.sprintlink.net!news.voicenet.com!netnews.
upenn.edu!cceb!sianFrom: siano@cceb.med.upenn.edu (Brian Siano)
Newsgroups: rec.arts.books.hist-fiction
Subject: Re: Roman Fiction
Date: 20 Sep 1995 04:03:12 GMT
Organization: University of Pennsylvania
Lines: 23
Message-ID: <43o3q0$o9v@netnews.upenn.edu>
References: <Pine.A32.3.91.950918223411.29218E-100000@acs5.acs.ucalgary.ca>
<tssmithDF68L2.5EL@netcom.com>
NNTP-Posting-Host: cceb.med.upenn.edu
X-Newsreader: TIN [version 1.2 PL2]

Tim Smith (tssmith@netcom.com) wrote:
: Blayne Robert Weidner <brweidne@acs.ucalgary.ca> writes:
: > Would any one be able to direct me to any historical fiction set
: >in ancient Rome. I have recently had to write a few essays about Rome
: >and would now prefer to read some fiction based in that era rather then
: >the nonfiction I was required to read. To anyone who replies, thank you
: >in advance.

: The two famous books of Robert Graves (_I, Claudius_ and _Claudius the God_)
: are the most well-known. There is also a set of videotapes available of
: the Claudius TV dramatizations. (These were broadcast in the USA about
: 10 years ago on PBS. They are British in origin. Excellent, especially
: Derek Jacoby's acting as Claudius, and Sian ?? as Livia.)

    If we're including novels about real events (not that I'm a
purist on the matter), then I'd also recommend Gore Vidal's _Julian_.
Basically a "memoir" about the Emperor who attempted to destroy the
burgeoning Christian church. Literate, well-written, enjoyable, and
basically Overall Good.

Name that book

This is a type of question that is directly beneficial to librarians. People frequently post requests for the identification of books that they have read before or heard described, and the collective memory of rec.arts.books is usually able to come up with the author and title.

Librarians can participate in these threads in two ways. We are often good at coming up with the right book, either from our own knowledge and experience or through the use of various Readers' Advisory tools. (And unlike most people posting to r.a.b., we usually provide a complete bibliographic citation!) Librarians can also place their own requests for patrons who can describe the entire plot for a book without giving you a single thing that could be used as a keyword.

What's a good book about . . . ?

Not all of the discussions on r.a.b. are literary; nonfiction of all types is also discussed. People often turn to the group for recommendations for good books on artificial intelligence, art history, and other topics.

Internet questions

People often post messages looking for other book-related resources : other USENET newsgroups, e-mail groups, the World Wide Web sites for various publishers, booksellers, etc., as well as those devoted to various authors or genres. New book-related resources are often posted as announcements to this group.

Gender issues

Are there women's books and men's books? Do men read books by women, and vice versa? Which male writers create convincing female characters, and vice versa? These and similar questions set off some lively debates.

Questions about Writing and Publishing

There are a number of aspiring writers who ask questions about the publishing process, agents, self-publishing, etc. Sometimes someone will post a message about how impossible it is to have really high quality fiction (i.e., theirs) published when the market is flooded with trash. This kind of message gets an immediate (i.e., empathetic) response.

Finding Books, Buying Books

Librarians are often surprised at the number of messages from people who need help with things we take for granted. There are many avid readers who apparently never use libraries and seem to have no idea of our services. Many have no idea how to find and use library catalogs, *Books in Print*, and other basic reference tools. It's also interesting to hear patrons explain interlibrary loan to each other.

Book clubs, ordering books by mail from publishers or from catalogs, and similar topics are frequently discussed. Rec.arts.books maintains excellent FAQ files on book clubs and Books by mail.

Even on the book groups, members sometimes explain ILL and other aspects of libraries, as seen on the following exchange on the Mercedes Lackey group:

FIGURE 5.4–5 Messages about Interlibrary Loan

Newsgroups: alt.books.m-lackey
Path:world!uunet!lin2.uu.net!news.sprintlink.net!howland.reston.ans.net!lamarck.sura.net!news.duc.
auburn.edu!mallard!caudlda
From: dillonda@vanderbilt.edu
8:51 GMT
Organization: Vanderbilt University
Lines: 39
Message-ID: <dillonda-2009951427170001@129.59.19.99>
NNTP-Posting-Host: 129.59.19.99
X-Newsreader: Yet Another NewsWatcher 2.0b27.5

I forget which thread this is officially from, but I figured I'd put my 2 cents in anyway.

Ordinarily I'd be chiming in with all those people complaining about the lack of certain books in their library. Especially since Vanderbilt's library doesn't have a great selection of the "good" books I want to read. (Good here only means what Vanderbilt calls "leisure reading": the contemporary popular books. They have plenty of classic literature and books on literature, etc.)

But I was pleasantly surprised to find Elvenblood on the shelves today - especially since it has recently been a topic of conversation here in this group. I didn't check it out today, because I have no leisure time this week to read a leisure book.

I would suggest to anyone whose library (for those of us who don't always want/have the ability to buy every book we want to read) doesn't have the book they are looking for to do one of the following:

1. See if they participate in the Inter-Library Loan program (ILL). Then if another library in your area has the book, they lend it to your library, and your library lends it to you! (It's amazing what you pick up when your mom is a librarian!)

OR

2. Become good friends with the person (or people) who order books for your library, suggest to them the books you want to read, and maybe they'll order it/them! (The problem with library collections, as I understand the situation from my mother, the librarian, is that they order what is most popular - the best sellers - or whatever the person who orders books happens to think might be interesting - because they don't really know what people want, they don't have ESP!) So if you tell your library that there is an interest in a book, they'll try to order it!

I hope this helps you understand why libraries don't always have the books you want - it's kinda like bookstores in a way - they have to have a potential market before they'll order the book!

Anyway, that's my 2 cents (or maybe a little more <grin>)

Deborah

FIGURE 5.4–5 (cont.)

Newsgroups: alt.books.m-lackey
Path:world!uunet!in2.uu.net!news.sprintlink.net!howland.reston.ans.net!lamarck.sura.net!news.duc.
auburn.edu!mallard!caudlda
From: caudlda@mail.auburn.edu (Dana Caudle)
Subject: Re: libraries and book availability
Message-ID: <DFA1EH.LvL@mail.auburn.edu>
Sender: usenet@mail.auburn.edu (Usenet Administrator)
Nntp-Posting-Host: mallard2.duc.auburn.edu
Organization: Auburn University
X-Newsreader: TIN [version 1.2 PL2]
References: <dillonda-2009951427170001@129.59.19.99>
Date: Thu, 21 Sep 1995 22:35:05 GMT
Lines: 24

Deborah Dillon (dillonda@ctrvax.vanderbilt.edu) wrote:
[Nice summary of ILL and library collection policies snipped.]
: I hope this helps you understand why libraries don't always have the books
: you want - it's kinda like bookstores in a way - they have to have a
: potential market before they'll order the book!

As a librarian, I can second everything Deborah said about ILL and telling
librarians what you want. But there are a couple of other reasons why the
library might not have Misty's books. First, of course, is funding.
Librarians try to buy as much as they can afford, but book prices have
soared in recent years. Journal (periodical) prices are even worse.
Plus, libraries are facing funding cuts as governments and universities
try to cut costs. Fiction tends to have a low priority, since it is more
likely than journals or nonfiction to be available to and purchased by the
general public through bookstores. Therefore, there is less demand. The
second reason is the type of library it is. As a general rule, college
and university libraries don't collect much fiction, period, preferring to
concentrate scarce resources on books and journals of scholarly value that
will provide more direct support to the university's mission. Public
libraries can justify a larger fiction budget as part of their mission.
[Shameless plug coming] Besides telling the librarians what you'd like to see,
support more funding for libraries. :-)

Dana

Films and Other Adaptations of Books

There are frequent discussions of movies and television adaptations of books, especially any changes to the story, which people on these lists generally dislike. The choice of actors to play different characters is always the source of much talk and disagreement, as people compare various actors with the characters they have pictured in their minds.

Books on cassette are also discussed here, with much debate on the issue of abridged versions versus full text recordings. R.a.b. people tend to be purists who disdain the abridgements.

Miscellaneous

How do you pronounce Ontdaaje? Where do ISBNs come from? Should bookstores shelve fiction by African-American authors in an African-American Studies area or integrate it into the fiction? How do you get rid of the musty smell from books that have been stored in the garage? How do you keep track of the books you have read? What's a good database program for cataloging the home library? What's the best age to teach a child to read? How can a parent who loves to read deal with a child who doesn't? Where can I get a list of bestsellers from fifty years ago? I saw an ad for a literary tour of the Lake Country; has anyone taken such a tour? What kind of reading lamp really prevents eyestrain?

If it has anything to do books, reading, or literary life in the broadest sense, it will appear on rec.arts.books and the other book-related USENET groups. The talk here tends to be lively and while members are generally helpful in answering each others requests there are also frequent disagreements. This contentiousness itself is also a common topic of conversation, as seen in the following r.a.b. exchange.

FIGURE 5.6 Agreeing to Disagree on rec.arts.books

Xref: world alt.culture.usenet:15594 rec.arts.books:144535
Path: world!news.kei.com!simtel!news.sprintlink.net!newsfeed.internetmci.com!nntp-
hub2.barrnet.net!news.Stanford.EDU!morrow.stanford.edu!pangea.Stanford.EDU!francis
From: francis@pangea.Stanford.EDU (Francis Muir)
Newsgroups: rec.arts.books,alt.culture.usenet
Subject: Re: RAB-weenies (Don't be...)
Date: 16 Sep 1995 21:45:29 GMT
Organization: Stanford Univ. Earth Sciences
Lines: 16
Message-ID: <43fghp$4i2@morrow.stanford.edu>
NNTP-Posting-Host: pangea.stanford.edu

Diane Carlson writes:

> I think it is perfectly legitimate to post that you hate an author,
> or disagree with a poster. This is just a healthy exchange of
> opinion. And it's a lot different from saying "so-an-so is a moronic
> troglodyte who must like killing small animals because he/she likes
> author 'X'..." I think you need to be a little less sensitive.

I must confess I enjoy people speaking their minds even if their minds are
not what they have most of. We will never see the nuclear family again, and
those who like myself grew up with six brothers and sisters are not altogether
sure that that is a particular misfortune. Here on rec.arts.books we are a
family of sorts and, luckily, there is no Nanny to instill the Wykhamist
mot, Manners Maketh the Man.

Fido

REC.ARTS.BOOKS.CHILDRENS

There are many discussions on rec.arts.books that touch on
children's literature, especially the conversations about the books
that changed your life, but there is now a separate newsgroup
that is devoted exclusively to children's literature. Although this
list includes many librarians, teachers, and authors and booksellers of children's books, it also includes many parents and others
who are just interested in the topic.

Here is a typical screen of messages on rec.arts.books.childrens:

FIGURE 5.7 Message Selection Screen on rec.arts.books.childrens

```
rec.arts.books.childrens (16T 21A 0K 0H R)          h=help

1 + 2      Fantasyland accessed by closet...???          susan howe check
2 +        EDWARD GOREY books wanted!                     http://www.amug.or
3 +        trying to remember book title                  Janet E. Rubin
4 + 2      Arthur Ransome books, help in finding please   Melissa Jan
5 +        New Totoro Homepage!                           Milky Way
6 +        Zilpha Keatly Snider                           Dawn Draheim
7 + 2      Willam Mayne                                   Maggie Burns
8 +        Need Feminst Book for 4 Year Old               Elaine Lawrence
9 +        Trina Schart Hyman / Cricket Magazine for      P HOLM63
10 +       Help me find this book!                        P HOLM63
11 +       Pop-up books                                   P HOLM63
12 +       Hubba-Hubba                                    P HOLM63
13 + 2     Need childrens books set in Caribbean          SDClark5
14 +       Poems for Beginners: Jack Prelutsky            Steve Cutchen
15 + 2     2nd Grade Title 1 Books                        Steve Cutchen
16 +       FREE PERSONALIZED SANTA LETTER +               Hayley Colina


<n>=set current to n, TAB=next unread, /=search pattern, ^K)ill/select,
a)uthor search, c)atchup, j=line down, k=line up, K=mark read, l)ist thread,
|=pipe, m)ail, o=print, q)uit, r=toggle all/unread, s)ave, t)ag, w=post

          *** End of Articles ***
```

One of the most common questions on this group is people wanting help identifying a book they remember from their own childhoods, which they would now like to reread, or perhaps to share with their own child. It's interesting to watch certain books recur as remembered yet forgotten, for example, "Many Moons" by James Thurber. It seems that many people spend years longing to find a certain book again, although often these are books that would be readily identifiable by any children's librarian.

Beyond the "identify-this-book" questions, there are many opportunities for people to discuss their favorites, sometimes remembered from childhood, sometimes recently reread, and often from recent experience with children. *The Wizard of Oz* series, *The Wind in the Willows*, *The Little House on the Prairies* series, *Swallows and Amazons*, the Elizabeth Enright books about the Melendy family, and everything by Madeline L'Engel and Beverly Cleary are frequently discussed.

There are also frequent discussions of all the old series' titles: Nancy Drew, the Hardy Boys, Honey Bunch, Maida, Sue Barton, the Rover Boys, and many others. These books are discussed by those who read and loved them as children, as well as those who see them as valuable collectibles now.

While people are lovingly discussing the old series books, another major discussion is disparaging various current series novels: everything by Christopher Pike and R.L. Stine, the Babysitters' Club books, the American Girls, etc.

Another common use of rec.arts.books.childrens is to look for recommendations for books for a child of a certain age or situation. What are good books for an eight-year-old who hates to read but loves sports, or for a child in a wheelchair, or for a child with a seriously ill parent? Children's librarians can both learn a great deal from these discussions and also make useful contributions.

Rec.arts.books.childrens is filled with reminders of how important reading is to children and how many adults still remember the books of their own early years. It's a great source of ideas, information, and even inspiration for children's librarians.

OTHER BOOK GROUPS

Rec.arts.books is a place to discuss all aspects of all types of books, and as such it is the most active of the book-related groups, but there are also many other groups on various types of books and individual authors. Some of these are rec.arts.books offshoots, with names that begin with r.a.b., but most are part of the alt.books or alt.fan hierarchy. Here is a list of book-related USENET newsgroups:

rec.arts.books	(All types of books)
rec.arts.books.childrens	(Children's books)
rec.arts.books.reviews	(Book reviews, moderated)
rec.arts.books.hist-fiction	(Historical fiction)
rec.arts.books.tolkien	(J.R.R. Tolkien)
alt.books.technical	(Technical books)
alt.books.reviews	(Book reviews)
alt.books.anne-rice	(Anne Rice)
alt.books.deryni	(Katherine Kurtz)
alt.books.isaac-asimov	(Isaac Asimov)
alt.books.m-lackey	(Mercedes Lackey)
alt.books.stephen-king	(Stephen King)
alt.books.tom-clancy	(Tom Clancy)
alt.books.sf.melanie-rawn	(Melanie Rawn)

alt.books.phil-k-dick	(Philip K. Dick)
alt.books.crichton	(Michael Crichton)
alt.fan.douglas-adams	(Douglas Adams)
alt.fan.eddings	(David Eddings)
alt.fan.pern	(Anne McCaffrey)

These single topic groups have discussions that are tightly focused on a particular author, although they sometimes drift into more general discussions of a genre, as people make comparisons between the author in question and others, or request suggestions for similar books by other authors. The Mercedes Lackey group, for example, often gets into general discussions of fantasy literature, and even maintains an extensive suggested reading list of books by other authors.

THE RABBERATTI: REFERENCE AND COLLECTION DEVELOPMENT

Rec.arts.books and the other book-related USENET groups can be a great source of information, as well as inspiration, for librarians. For reference, the ability to tap into the collective knowledge of the groups is an invaluable aid in identifying a book from the limited information that our patrons are sometimes able to give us.

The groups can also be a great help in collection development. Just observing the group discussion is a good way to learn more about the preferences and habits of some very active and articulate readers. Checking your collection against some of the books discussed is a good way to find gaps in your collection, especially older titles that may have been lost but are still in demand.

The discussion is not limited to fiction, and you'll find many recommendations for books on a wide variety of subject areas, from art to sports. One of the groups, alt.books.technical, is an especially good source of information for those trying to keep up with the great flood of books about the Internet!

6 JUST THE FAQS

Many people participate in on-going conversations on USENET and other online forums, but over time, these conversations tend to become repetitive. In order to reduce the amount of repetition and help newcomers understand how the group works, many groups have developed FAQs, files of Frequently Asked Questions (and their answers!). These files are not only helpful to people joining a discussion group, they are valuable information resources for people with an interest in the topic and for librarians helping people locate information in the area.

PERIODIC POSTINGS

Many of the most interesting online communities, especially the USENET groups, maintain FAQ files. These provide general information about the group and the answers to questions that have come up on the group time and time again. This both provides a service to the newcomers, by answering many of their questions, and keeps the group from becoming too repetitive for the regulars. This is especially important on the USENET newsgroups, because USENET's bulletin board format encourages new people to join different groups frequently, dropping in and out for short periods of time. Another factor for the rapid turnover in groups, of course, is the rapid increase in the number of people with USENET access, bringing many new participants to most of the groups. E-mail groups tend to be smaller and have a more stable membership, and fewer have real FAQ files, although some list owners have written extensive welcome files, (introductory messages sent to new subscribers), that include some of the same material as the USENET FAQs.

The USENET FAQs are usually the work of a volunteer who solicits ideas from the group, or sometimes simply posts a draft. This usually happens after certain questions elicit almost an audible groan, and participants start mentioning the need for a FAQ. Once the first version of the FAQ is posted, other people will suggest possible revisions, corrections, and additional topics. In order to serve its primary purpose of assisting newcomers to the group, the FAQ needs to be reposted to the newsgroup frequently, usually once or twice a month. This ensures that the FAQ will always be available on most USENET sites, which usually only keep two to four weeks' worth of new messages.

The frequent repostings as well as additions and changes made by group members create an environment of constant revision, and as the FAQs develop, they often divide into a series of individual files or articles dealing with different aspects of a topic. These articles, collectively known as Periodic Postings, represent a new type of publishing. Periodic Postings are fluid documents, always in progress, never complete, and are communal works, maintained by one person (often called the "FAQ-keeper"), but are really the creation and intellectual property of the group.

ANATOMY OF A FAQ

Frequently Asked Questions have become an important part of USENET culture and a certain standard format has evolved. Each FAQ generally includes certain standard information about the FAQ itself, either at the beginning or end of the file. This includes information about the compiler of the file and others who have contributed to it, the posting schedule, information on where the file is archived, and how to obtain current copies by FTP and mail-server. It's now becoming common to list the locations of different versions of the FAQ, such as plain ASCII text and hypertext.

Now that the Internet has become big business, most FAQ-keepers are adding certain legal information to their files. This now generally means a notice of copyright and a statement granting certain rights of distribution and forbidding others. This usually means giving permission to distribute the file freely over the Internet, as long as it is kept intact, but forbidding any for-profit reproduction.

Several companies have gathered all the FAQs from public archives and sold them on CD-ROMs, a practice that has angered many FAQ-keepers. One collection development issue that this raises is that while CD-ROM distribution makes the valuable information in the FAQs available to many people without Internet access, FAQs on CD-ROM are quickly outdated, unlike the frequently reposted and updated FAQs on USENET or the Internet archives. However, to quote Russell Hersch in the FAQ on FAQs,

"The basic objection to the use of FAQs without the permission of the author, is one of control over copyrighted material. The FAQ maintainer works hard at compiling and maintaining the FAQ. The issue is not one of greed, since it is clear that the FAQ maintainer wants to share with others. It just isn't fair for someone else to make a buck at it."[1]

Another common practice is to include a disclaimer, a statement designed to discourage lawsuits. Disclaimers state that although the information is believed to be accurate, the FAQ-keeper can't be held responsible for any adverse effects of using the information. Many FAQs, especially in the medical, legal and financial areas, remind the reader of the importance of professional advice, as in this example from misc.invest.funds:

DISCLAIMER:

> This question and answer list is given in the hope that it is useful, but with no express or implied warranty for accuracy, usefulness, up-to-dateness, or anything else. Use the information contained in this list at your own risk. Before investing in any mutual fund, be sure to read the latest prospectus for the fund in its entirety. This FAQ should NOT be used in place of competent advice from investment, accounting and legal professionals. This FAQ applies to mutual funds in the USA - most things are likely to differ elsewhere.[2]

FAQs generally include three types of information: guidelines for the group, questions about the subject area, and pointers to other sources of information.

GUIDELINES

The guidelines for the group define the scope of the group's subject area and general principles of netiquette. They may differentiate the group from other related groups, and include reminders relevant to the group, such as the policy on advertising items for sale or wanted to buy. Most groups also advise members from the practice of flaming, the standard net term for posting personal attacks in response to controversial postings.

The following is an example of the group guidelines from rec.skiing.snowboard:

Here are a few rules of thumb that will help you get around in rec.skiing.snowboard (and even some other places) without firmly inserting your foot in your mouth.

- Don't quote entire articles. Only quote what is absolutely necessary in order to make your point clear. Anytime you are quoting more than you're writing you should question yourself.
- Avoid long signature files. They may look cool the first time you see one but they get real old real quick.

- Limit lines to 80 characters *max*, preferably 68-72 chars. If you don't, whatever you write will be very difficult for a lot of people to read because the lines will get broken-up and segmented.
- You're probably better off if you avoid telling everybody what a radical snowboarder you are.
- rec.skiing.snowboard is populated by some "unique" individuals. You'll notice a lot of people making fun of various ski areas, various techniques, and various other people. Don't go taking all of this seriously! For the most part there are a lot of tongues firmly inserted in cheeks.
- There *will* be flame wars from time to time. Try not to take these too seriously either; they rarely get hot enough to actually melt the snow.[3]

THE QUESTIONS THEMSELVES

Of course, the most important part of the FAQ is the Frequently Asked Questions themselves and their answers. These questions and answers are very useful to librarians, since they are probably the same ones that come up at the reference desk on the topic of the newsgroup.

The question-and-answer format of the FAQs fits in well with reference work. The answers that are included in the FAQs are generally reliable, accurate, and current, since they are subjected to constant peer review from the group. In fact, they sometimes point out errors or contradictions in published sources.

What kind of information is in the FAQs? The rec.bicycles FAQ tells how to make milk jug mud flaps, how to adjust chains, and where to buy "One Less Car" t-shirts. The rec.boats.paddle FAQ explains river ratings. The rec.arts.comic FAQ explains the different types of Kryptonite, and answers the question, "How do you spell/pronounce the last name of artist Bill Sienkiewicz?" Harmonet, an e-mail group devoted to Barbershop singing, has a FAQ which gives the address of the Sweet Adelines, a women's barbershop organization. The rec.music.classical FAQ gives a list of the classical music used in movies and television, (including the Acura commercial) although, it explains, "We have a little joke in the newsgroup that no matter what movie or TV show, it's probably either Pachelbel's Canon or Carmina Burana." The Quaker FAQ explains the proper use of the words "thee" and "thou." The sci.physics FAQ has explanations and citations for various science puzzlers, including why "Hot water freezes faster than cold."

A look at the list of questions for one of the groups will give you a better idea of the kind of questions that are covered. This is the list of questions from the Coffee and Caffeine FAQ, maintained by Alejandro Lopez-Ortiz:

1. The Chemistry of Caffeine and related products
   1. How much caffeine is there in [drink/food/pill]?
   2. How much caffeine is there in blend X?
   3. Chemically speaking, what is caffeine?
   4. Is it true that tea has no caffeine/What is theine, theobromine, etc?
   5. Where can I find a gif of the caffeine molecule?
   6. Is it true that espresso has less caffeine than regular coffee?
   7. How does caffeine taste?
   8. How much theobromine/theophylline is there in . . . ?
2. How to brew the ultimate caffeine drink?
   1. What is the best temperature for drip coffee?
   2. Quality of coffee
   3. Why you should never use percolators
3. Peripherals and Secondary Storage
   1. Proper care of Coffee makers . . .
   2. How to store coffee?
   3. Equipment reviews?
   4. What is a French Press/Cafetiere/Bodum?
4. Caffeine and your Health
   1. Caffeine Withdrawal
   2. What happens when you overdose?
   3. Effects of caffeine on pregnant women.
   4. Caffeine and Osteoporosis (Calcium loss)
   5. Studies on the side-effects of caffeine . . .
   6. Caffeine and depression.
   7. Caffeine and your metabolism.
5. Miscellaneous
   1. How do you pronounce mate?
   2. How do you spell Colombia/Colombian?
   3. How do you spell Espresso?
6. Coffee Recipes and other beverages.
   1. Espresso
   2. Chocolate covered espresso beans
   3. Cappuccino
   4. Frappe
   5. How to make your own chocolate
   6. How to make the best cup of coffee
   7. Turkish Coffee
   8. Irish Coffee
   9. Thai Iced Coffee
   10. Vietnamese Iced Coffee
   11. Melya
7. Administrivia
   1. List of Contributors
   2. Copyright[4]

The FAQs are also great for "proactive reference," providing answers to questions that people haven't asked. You can print out some of the FAQs and give them to patrons or local groups with a special interest in a subject. This is a great way to promote the value of both the Internet and librarians. If your library is developing a World Wide Web page to provide Internet access to patrons, make sure you provide a direct route to some of the FAQs on some of the subject areas you know will interest patrons, as a sort of browsing collection.

One group that will really appreciate this is young adults. Because so many USENET participants are college students, there is especially good coverage of subjects of interest to young people. There are excellent FAQs for many popular music groups such as the one for the alternative group They Might Be Giants. In addition to giving the history of the group and a discography, it explains various allusions in the music, from the death of Phil Ochs to the Lucille Ball movie, "The Long, Long Trailer." There is also an extensive series of files on Inline Skating, which is one of the best guides to this subject.

POINTERS TO OTHER SOURCES

The last section of the FAQs includes pointers to all sorts of other resources: organizations, competitions, events, support groups, and sources of supplies, as well as other Internet resources. This is also great reference material, including sources for large size clothing (alt.support.big-folks), nonleather shoes (rec.food.vegetarian), patterns for historic clothing (rec.crafts.sewing), pet doors, (rec.pets.dogs) and bonsai supplies (rec.bonsai). The sources listed here are often small, specialty businesses that are difficult to find in other types of directories.

The FAQs almost always include a list of recommended books, and these lists are unique resources for collection development. Here you will find the books that are recommended by people who share a serious interest in a particular field. These lists often include old books as well as new ones, and some small press or specialty books that librarians might miss otherwise.

Most groups start out with a single FAQ file that includes all of the elements listed here. Eventually, as the FAQ grows, it may be divided, with certain sections becoming separate files. The resources lists (for example, lists of suppliers) and the booklists are the most likely candidates for separate lists. Once the booklist becomes a separate file, it often grows in length and complexity. The "Publications" Periodic Postings for rec.pets.dogs, for example, is divided into the following sections:

Publications
A. Addressing Behavior Problems
B. Annual Publications
C. Books on Canine Health & Care
D. Breed Information Books
E. Canine Behavior
F. Dogs and the Law
G. Dog Stories
H. General Care
I. Herding
J. Miscellaneous
K. Obedience Training
L. Puppies
M. Research Articles on Canine Health
N. Search and Rescue
O. Service Dogs
P. Sled Dogs
Q. Tracking or Trailing: Scenting
R. Training Hunting Dogs
S. Working Dogs (other)[5]

The Dog Publications FAQ is a prime example of a well-developed booklist. The books listed are given complete citations, including ISBNs, and many are annotated. Here's an example:

> Zink, M. Christine, DVM, PHD. _Peak Performance: Coaching the
>   Canine Athlete_.*Howell Book House, 1992. ISBN: 0-87605-757-1.
> This eminently readable book goes over canine physiology, both internal and structural. She covers how to keep your dog in general good shape, discusses some conditioning strategies, and finally details a number of possible impediments to conditioning your dog, including: genetic and traumatic joint problems and lameness, the effects of medication on your dog, and moreover lists all the things you need to consider when trying to keep your dog fit and healthy. Recommended for all people doing regular physical activity with their dog.[6]

The publications article is the work of master FAQ-keeper Cindy Tittle Moore, who also maintains many other of the pets FAQs as well as many of the rec.arts.books FAQs. These have now been rewritten to HTML, the markup language of the World Wide Web, and they are all available from her home page, (URL://http://www.zmall.com/pet_talk/tittle/).

Most booklists aren't as long or well-organized as the dogs one, but still contain useful information. The booklists compiled by the newsgroups often present a different view of the literature than standard, professional reviewing sources, and may be viewed

---

*The underscore characters at the beginning and end of the title indicate italicizing, which is not possible in e-mail or Listservs.

as "the people's choice" in any subject area. For example, there is a Depression Booklist that is compiled from the USENET newsgroup alt.support.depression, the e-mail group Walkers in Darkness, and the Mood Disorders Support Network on America Online. These recommendations are not necessarily the same books that professionals feel should be helpful to the depressed, they are books that depressed people recommend to each other.

One way that librarians can contribute to the Internet community is to participate in the creation, maintenance, and development of FAQs and other Periodical Postings. We have the skills and resources to track down and verify the answers to frequently asked questions, and to provide complete citations for references. We also have a natural talent for the organization and arrangement of information which makes us ideally suited to suggest and create new resources. The interest groups have much to offer librarians, but when we drop in to use these resources, we should also contribute to their development.

HOW TO FIND THE FAQS AND OTHER PERIODIC POSTINGS

The FAQs can be found all over the Internet, using every method of information retrieval. Although they were originally tightly associated with a single USENET newsgroup, many are now posted to several related groups, and can be found through Gophers and World Wide Web sites. In fact, FAQs have become one of the most important sources of information content on the Internet.

USENET

If you have USENET access, you will run across the Periodic Postings all the time, posted to their own newsgroups. You can also find them posted to the special "*.answers" newsgroups, which exist solely as a repository for periodic postings. Each hierarchy has its own "answers" group, so you can look in rec.answers for all the periodic postings from the rec groups, soc.answers for all the postings from the soc groups, etc. News.answers has the postings for all the hierarchies, and serves as a USENET version of a vast, totally disorganized, vertical file. Checking the subject lines of this group occasionally is a great way to keep an eye on USENET and is an aid to serendipity, one of the great underrated reference tools. Serendipity is finding things you weren't looking for, and USENET is great for that.

ANONYMOUS FTP

All the Periodic Postings are archived at the FTP site rtfm.mit.edu. MIT is the Massachusetts Institute of Technology, and the server name "rtfm" is a techie inside joke, a reference to the most frequent answer to technical questions, "Read the F'ing Manual."

If you have access to anonymous FTP, you can connect to rtfm.mit.edu and go to the directory "/pub/usenet/news.answers" where you will find all of the periodic postings. If you are using a graphical World Wide Web browser such as Netscape, try entering the URL "ftp://rtfm.mit.edu" as an easy way to do anonymous FTP.

E-MAIL

If you only have e-mail access to the Internet, you can still retrieve files from rtfm through MIT's mail-server. To get a listing of the periodic postings for a particular newsgroup, send the command "index/[newsgroup] to mail-server@rtfm.mit.edu." For example:

```
To:        mail-server@rtfm.mit.edu
Subject:   [leave blank]
index/rec.arts.books/
```

The files will be listed in your return message, and you can request the files by sending the message "send usenet/[newsgroup]/[filename]". For example,

```
To:        mail-server@rtfm.mit.edu
Subject:
send usenet/rec.arts.books/books.by.mail
```

For more information getting periodic postings via e-mail, send the command "help" to mail-server@rtfm.mit.edu.

GOPHER AND WORLD WIDE WEB

Even if you don't have USENET access, you will find the periodic postings all over the Internet. When you use Gopher or your Web browser, your client program is actually using FTP to retrieve the files for you, and you generally will have some way of downloading them, printing them, or mailing them to yourself. Once you know the name of a particular file, you can usually find it by using any search utility, such as Veronica for Gopher and Lycos or WebCrawler for the World Wide Web.

One invaluable resource is Tom Fine's Internet Answers Collection, http://www.smartpages.com/faqs/. This is a World Wide Web site developed by Thomas A. Fine of Ohio State University, using software he designed to extract all the FAQs from news.answers and convert them to HTML, the language of the World Wide Web. The software looks for URLs and converts them into active links, making every FAQ a Web page filled with links to other resources.

The FAQs play an important role on the Internet, because they are generally available for free redistribution, unlike the text of magazine articles, selections from books, and other regular, published material.

LIBRARIANS AND THE FAQS

Librarians will find the FAQs to be an invaluable source of answers, since they tend to cover the same questions that are frequently asked in libraries. Taken together, they are, in effect, a giant reference database of questions and answers, and one that is constantly being revised and expanded.

The FAQs have grown far beyond just the answers to individual questions, as they have developed considerable lists of other resources, including subject-oriented guides to the Internet, lists of organizations, newsletters, catalogs, stores and more, all of which can be very useful for reference work.

The lists of books are particularly interesting to librarians doing collection development. While book reviews are the opinion of one person, based on an initial reading of a book, the Internet lists are communal, the recommendations of many people, based on all their experiences using particular books. You might call them booklists "of the people, by the people, and for the people."

NOTES

1. Hersch, Russell. "FAQs about FAQs" [World Wide Web] http://www.cis.ohio-state.edu/hypertext/faq/usenet/about-faqs/faq.html (14 Feb. 1996)
2. Mark, Randy. "Frequently Asked Questions (FAQ) for Misc.invest.funds" (v. 2.3) [World Wide Web] http://www.cis.

ohio-state.edu/hypertext/faq/usenet/investment-faq/mutual-funds/faq.html (14 Feb 1996)

3. Wallace, Mark. "The Snowboarding FAQ" [World Wide Web] http://www.nyx.net/~mwallace/sb_faq.html (14 Feb. 1996)

4. Lopez-Ortiz, Alejandro. "Coffee and Caffeine's Frequently Asked Questions" (v. 2.95) [World Wide Web] http://daisy.uwaterloo.ca/~alopez-o/caffaq.html (14 Feb. 1996)

5. Moore, Cindy Tittle. "Rec.pets.dogs: Publications FAQ" [World Wide Web] http://www.zmall.com/pet_talk/tittle/pets/dog_faqs/publications.html (14 Feb. 1996)

6. Ibid.

7 GOPHER AND THE WORLD WIDE WEB

GOPHER

Before Gopher was introduced in 1991, Internet users were generally limited to using the basic Internet protocols of telnet, FTP, and e-mail, as well as USENET where it was available. Using the Internet required training and experience, and generally a willingness to learn a little UNIX. Most Internet users were connected with colleges and universities, and, of necessity, all were computer-literate.

Gopher, an easy Internet interface that anyone could quickly learn to use, opened up the Internet to many more people. Gopher works on hierarchical menus. Before Gopher, if you wanted to connect to another system, you needed to enter the telnet command and the telnet address. This meant that you needed to know the telnet address, so Internet users accumulated lots of scraps of paper and spent a lot of time trying to find addresses. With Gopher, if you want to connect to the online catalog of the library at Boston University, you go through a series of menus, with names like "Online Library Catalogs," "Massachusetts," and find the entry for Boston University. When you find the entry and hit "Enter," the telnet connection is made. When you exit from the catalog, you are back on the Gopher.

With Gopher, you don't need to know the telnet address because the Gopher behind every menu item is a Gopher link, a file with the address and retrieval information for the item. The Gopher organizes and stores information, and makes the connection, not unlike programming memory buttons on your phone.

In addition to making telnet connections, Gopher can retrieve files through FTP. This means that instead of having to know the FTP address and working your way through the arcane directory structure on someone else's computer to get a copy of "The Declaration of Independence," you could browse through a Gopher menu called "Historical Documents," find a listing for it, hit "Enter" and have it displayed on your screen. If you wanted a copy of the document, you could have the Gopher save it, download it, mail it, or print it.

A reference librarian might use a Gopher to help a patron who is looking for sources of patterns for historic costuming, starting from a typical Gopher main menu, as seen using the Unix Gopher client:

FIGURE 7.1 Gopher Main Menu, Seen Through the UNIX Gopher Client

```
          Internet Gopher Information Client v2.1.3

          Home Gopher server: gopher.noble.mass.edu

     1.  NOBLE : North of Boston Library Exchange/
     2.  MLIN Gopher/
     3.  Massachusetts Resources/
     4.  Reference/
 --> 5.  Arts, Sports and Recreation/
     6.  Business, Jobs, Economics and Statistics/
     7.  Education/
     8.  Environment and Ecology/
     9.  Geography, History and Social Sciences/
    10.  Government and Law/
    11.  Health and Home/
    12.  Language and Literature/
    13.  Librarianship/
    14.  Math, Science and Technology/
    15.  Philosophy, Psychology and Religion/
    16.  The Internet : Information, Search Tools, and Other Gateways/
    17.  Weather, News, and Seasonal/
    18.  The NOBLE Children's Library/

Press ? for Help, q to Quit                            Page: 1/1
```

Gopher uses item types to distinguish between different types of menu items. In the Unix Gopher client, an item with no mark at the end indicates a file, a slash (/) indicates a directory (another menu), and the symbol <?> indicates a search.

Selecting *Arts, Sports and Recreation* from this menu gets us another menu—

FIGURE 7.2 Secondary Gopher Menu

```
                    Internet Gopher Information Client v2.1.3

                        Arts, Sports and Recreation

          1.  Alt.art.ballet FAQ/
          2.  Aquanaut (SCUBA Forum) <HTML>
          3.  Bicycling/
          4.  Bonsai FAQ <HTML>
          5.  Canoe, Kayak, Raft and PaddleSports/
          6.  Cartoons, Comics and Graphic Novels/
          7.  Counted Cross Stitch FAQ <HTML>
          8.  Fencing FAQ <HTML>
          9.  LEGO FAQ <HTML>
          10. Model Railroad FAQ <HTML>
          11. Movies/
          12. Music/
          13. Photography/
    -->   14. Sewing and Textiles/
          15. Skydiving FAQ <HTML>
          16. Sports/
          17. Standup Comedy FAQ <HTML>
          18. Television/

Press ? for Help, q to Quit                              Page: 1/1
```

And selecting *Sewing and Textiles* from that menu gets us another menu—

FIGURE 7.3 Another Gopher Menu

```
                    Internet Gopher Information Client v2.1.3

                           Sewing and Textiles

        -->   1.  Historical Costuming FAQ
              2.  Textiles FAQ
              3.  Textiles Related Books FAQ, Part 1/2
              4.  Textiles Related Books FAQ, Part 2/2
```

And selecting from that menu gets us what we want—The Historical Costuming FAQ, a document that is regularly posted to a number of newsgroups related to sewing, crafts, theatre, and the Society for Creative Anachronism.

FIGURE 7.4 File Retrieved by Gopher

```
Historical Costuming FAQ (47k)                                          1%

Historical Costuming FAQ

From: lara@sgi.sgi.com
Newsgroups: alt.sewing,rec.crafts.textiles.sewing,rec.arts.theatre.stagecraft,re
c.crafts.textiles.misc,rec.org.sca,news.answers,alt.answers,rec.answers
Subject: Historical Costuming FAQ
Supersedes: <cost_807835015@yorgi.csd.sgi.com>
Followup-To: rec.crafts.textiles.misc
Date: 27 Sep 1995 14:33:44 GMT
Organization: Silicon Graphics, Inc, Mountain View, CA
Lines: 1254
Approved: news-answers-request@MIT.Edu
Distribution: world
Expires: 30 Nov 1995 14:33:19 GMT
Message-ID: <cost_812212399@yorgi.csd.sgi.com>
Reply-To: lara@sgi.sgi.com
NNTP-Posting-Host: yorgi.csd.sgi.com
Summary: Lists of sources for patterns and supplies for historical costuming.
         Bibliography of relevant books.  Info relevant to SCA periods (600 AD

[Help: ?]  [Exit: u]  [PageDown: Space]
```

Like most FAQs, the first screen of this one is a daunting display of technical information about the FAQ and its posting schedule. Once we get beyond that, however, we would find a lot of useful information on historical costumes for our patron.

Gopher organizes the Internet resources and makes the actual connections needed to bring a copy of this file to our computer. The selection of resources on a Gopher, and the way resources are divided and the names and organization of the menus depends on how the local Gopher administrator set up the Gopher server.

In addition to menus and files, Gopher can handle searches by collecting search terms and sending them off to a database server. These databases are often handy for ready reference. For example, if a patron phones with a question regarding stain removal, we could go to a Gopher menu item that looks like this:

Search the HomeCare Database <?>

Choosing this menu item gives us a window where we can enter search terms. These terms are sent to the remote server and a menu of matching record is returned:

FIGURE 7.5 Results from the HomeCare Database Search

```
          Internet Gopher Information Client v2.1.3

        Search HomeCare Database (spill/stains on surface): mustard

-->  1.  Mustard : Furniture
     2.  Mustard : Porches, Decks, Patios
     3.  Mustard : Siding/Walls
     4.  Mustard : Hard Surface Floors
     5.  Mustard : Washable Apparel
     6.  Mustard : Walls and Ceilings
     7.  Mustard : Other/Interior
     8.  Mustard : Carpet
     9.  Mustard : Upholstered Furniture




Press ? for Help, q to Quit                           Page: 1/1
```

The HomeCare Database is located at the Cooperative Extension Service of the North Carolina State University, but you don't need to know that. Any Gopher server can have this item on the menu, transmit searches, and display the results.

GOPHER HISTORY

The name Gopher was a reference to the Golden Gopher, the mascot at the University of Minnesota, where the Gopher was developed. There's an additional punning reference to the term *gofer*, someone whose job is to go for this and go for that, which is pretty much what the Internet Gopher does for its users. The Gopher imagery of Gopher holes and Gopher tunnels in the vast, interconnected world of Gopherspace has helped many people visualize the concept of global distributed information resources.

Like most things on the Internet, Gopher is a client/server application. The Gopher client is a piece of software that sits on your computer and works on your behalf. The Gopher client shows you menus and files, handles connections and transfers, and takes care of tasks such as mailing and downloading files. The Gopher server, which can be anywhere in the world, is a hierarchical set of menus that can be accessed by any Gopher client. Most Gopher servers are a combination of files and other resources on the local system as well as pointers to resources on other Gopher servers. Any Gopher client can reach any Gopher server, including the University of Minnesota's list of all Gopher servers.

Gopher's easy menu access to resources contributed to the burst of Internet growth in the early 1990s, making the Internet accessible to users who would not have been willing to memorize commands and transcribe complex addresses. It was the Internet's first successful organizing tool because it enabled people to explore the Internet by browsing.

Since any Gopher can point to resources on other Gophers, the world called Gopherspace quickly became very complex. The hierarchical structure of Gopher servers imposes order, but this order can also be rigid and confining.

After a few brief years of glory, Gopher lost its role as the primary means for organizing and presenting information on the Internet. The World Wide Web, which had been around for some time, became an overnight success due to the introduction of Mosaic, a powerful, friendly client program. The most important of Mosaic's novel features was its ability to handle graphics. Although PC Gopher clients could display graphics, Mosaic allowed graphics and text and links to open resources to be integrated into a single display. Suddenly everyone wanted Mosaic's point-and-click, full color Internet access. Although Gopher is a good way of organizing and presenting certain types of material, and still remains a powerful force on the Internet, most development of new resources is taking place on the World Wide Web.

WHAT IS THE WORLD WIDE WEB?

The World Wide Web consists of clients and servers on computers around the Internet which exchange information through HTTP, the Hypertext Transfer Protocol. The biggest difference between Gopher and the Web is the basic unit of organization.

- Gopher works on a series of hierarchical menus. This method of presenting information is logical and orderly, but can also be rigid and dull.
- The World Wide Web is based on hypertext, a technique that connects files to each other through links that can be followed or skipped at the choice of the viewer.

To some extent, printed works have used a primitive hypertext-like arrangement all along. Most books are written with the presumption that you will read every chapter, and read them in order. Footnotes or endnotes, however, are links to additional, optional information, and you can skip right over them as you read, or choose to "follow the link" if there is a note for a quotation you find particularly striking or a statistic that you find difficult to believe. Encyclopedias and similar works often use links from one article to another, either by listing related articles at the end of an article, or by noting relevant articles from within the text itself.

That element of choice, allowing the reader to make decisions and control their exploration of the text, is the essence of hypertext. The concept may be old, but the powerful ability of computers to quickly and seamlessly move you from one document or image to another has made hypertext an integral—and expected—basic part of today's information systems. CD-ROM encyclopedias, for example, base much of their appeal on the ability to jump from article to article by following links. CD-ROM encyclopedias also add graphics and sound, so that you can not only read about the Battle of Gettysburg, but also see photographs and perhaps hear "The Battle Hymn of the Republic." With the addition of sound, graphics, and other formats beyond the printed word, hypertext becomes hypermedia!

The World Wide Web expands the concept of hypermedia far beyond the world of the CD-ROM encyclopedia, by linking text, sound, and graphics, on any computer anywhere in the world that is also part of the World Wide Web.

WORLD WIDE WEB BROWSER PROGRAMS

The World Wide Web works on the client/server model, with a client program on your computer acting as your interface to the Web. Depending on the nature of your Internet connection, you may be using a browser program on your desktop computer, or a browser on the computer that you are connected to, either as a terminal or by dialing into a shell account.

There are many different browser programs available for the PC. Mosaic, the browser that brought so much attention to the World Wide Web, is still popular, but its dominance has been eclipsed by Netscape, a commercial product. America Online and other commercial online services use their own proprietary browser programs.

Lynx, available from the University of Kansas where it was developed, is the most popular browser program for Unix and VMS systems. Lynx is a textual browser only, it can't handle graphics, but is the best World Wide Web browser for use with terminals connected over serial lines to a central computer or those with dial-in shell accounts to the Internet. This includes a large number of libraries and librarians, who have Internet access through computer and telecommunications systems that were designed to handle circulation systems and online public access catalogs, both traditionally terminal-based applications.

Lynx is also the browser program usually used by visually impaired people. Lynx has an option that displays numbers for each link. Working with voice programs that read the screen, the visually impaired user can navigate the World Wide Web by using the number keys on their PC or terminal.

THERE'S NO PLACE LIKE HOME PAGE

The development of the World Wide Web is one of the most significant developments in the history of the Internet as a populist information utility. E-mail groups and USENET newsgroups developed a whole culture of many-to-many communication, where any individual with the right connection could communicate with many other people simultaneously. This was a sharp contrast to the world of publishing and broadcasting, which is few-to-many communication, and is actually a throwback to the tradition of the open forum or town meeting, where everyone can speak as equals.

However, while e-mail groups and USENET were providing many-to-many communication, other Internet services were still primarily on the few-to-many model. Internet connectivity allows many systems to offer services such as telnet access to library catalogs, and for larger organizations to offer information through Gopher. With the World Wide Web, however, anyone with an account on a system running a Web server (and permission to do so) can easily create their own set of information, available to everyone on the Web.

It's easy to create a World Wide Web Home Page, which can be a single document, marked up in HTML. Many people are creating home pages for themselves and their organizations. Others are creating sites devoted to particular subject areas, combining locally created resources with links to other resources located around the Internet.

HTML: THE LANGUAGE OF THE WEB

In order to understand the tremendous proliferation of activity on the World Wide Web, it helps to have a basic understanding of HTML, the language of the Web.

The basic unit of the World Wide Web is the page, a single document written with HTML, Hypertext Markup Language. Each page is an ASCII text document that is marked up using the HTML's codes, called *tags*, to designate the structure of the information presented. HTML does not determine the specific appearance of the page, which will vary according to the browser used and options selected.

Creating HTML Documents

HTML documents are simple ASCII text files, and can be created using any type of text editing or word processing program. There are many special programs for writing HTML or for converting existing text to HTML, some of which are shareware and some of which are commercial programs. These can be a convenience and can provide some verification of format, but you don't need a special program to write or edit basic HTML. Templates for basic home pages can be found around the Web, and on software included with many HTML books.

Common HTML Tags

Most HTML tags come in pairs, to start and end a particular attribute. For example, there are a few tags that designate major sections of a document: <HTML></HTML> to enclose the document as a whole, <HEAD></HEAD> and <BODY></BODY> to designate the heading from the body of the document, and <TITLE></TITLE> to designate the title within the HEAD.

The other common tags designate heading levels: <H1></H1>, <H2></H2>, etc. These tags are interpreted in some consistent style by the browser. For example, a browser may present H1s as centered and in a larger font, H2s as left justified and in a somewhat smaller font, etc.

List tags are commonly used to designate unordered lists <UL> or ordered lists <OL>. Unordered lists are generally displayed with bullets, and ordered lists with numbers. The paragraph tags, <P></P>, are used to enclose plain text paragraphs. There are special tags that designate style, for example, <EM></EM> for emphasis (usually italics) and <STRONG></STRONG> for greater emphasis (usually bold).

Images

The image and link tags are different than the paired, formatting tags. The image tag retrieves an image file and displays it as part of the page, and the link tag retrieves and displays another page.

The image needs an attribute that is the location of the image file. For example, if I am writing the Abraham Lincoln home page, I might have a picture of Lincoln in a file called lincoln.gif, and my image tag would look like this <IMG SRC="lincoln.gif">. There is another important attribute for all image tags, called the ALT or alternate attribute. This allows you to specify text that will be displayed if the graphic cannot be displayed. My Lincoln tag might be
<IMG SRC="lincoln.gif" ALT="Abraham Lincoln">.

If the ALT attribute is not used, the image displays as [IMAGE], which is confusing to users of nongraphical browsers, people with their Autoload images feature turned off, and blind users who have software reading the screen.

Links

The link tag is used to move the user to another page, which can be on the same server, or anywhere else on the Web. These are usually referred to as internal and external links. For example, if I were doing a home page for my library, I might create separate documents for the library hours, library policies, and the services of various departments of the library. I would create internal links to these documents. I might also include external links to relevant other World Wide Web home pages, for example, the Library of Congress, state and local government resources, etc.

The link tag looks like this:

Internal: <A HREF="reference">
(pointing to a file called "reference" in my home directory)
External: <A HREF="http://www.loc.gov>"
(pointing to a URL elsewhere on the Web)

SCRIPTS, FORMS, AND MAILTO LINKS

Many browsers can now handle scripts, forms, and mailto links. These three elements allow us to create Web sites that go beyond being displays of text, images, and other media, and create interactive sites that can provide an array of services.

Scripts

Scripts are gateways between the Web page and other programs. A simple script would be to have the date and time appear on the page, by using a script that does a date/time command on the host system. Another common script displays the number of times the page has been viewed. Scripts can be used to gather and process all types of information, providing that the background scripts exist. The term CGI (Common Gateway Interface) is often used to refer to scripting, although technically this refers to the interface between the page and a Unix system.

Another interesting use of scripts can be seen at the Web site of the Saint Joseph County Public Library. Their Web page offers access to the library's file of difficult reference questions.

FIGURE 7.6 Saint Joseph County Public Library Info File

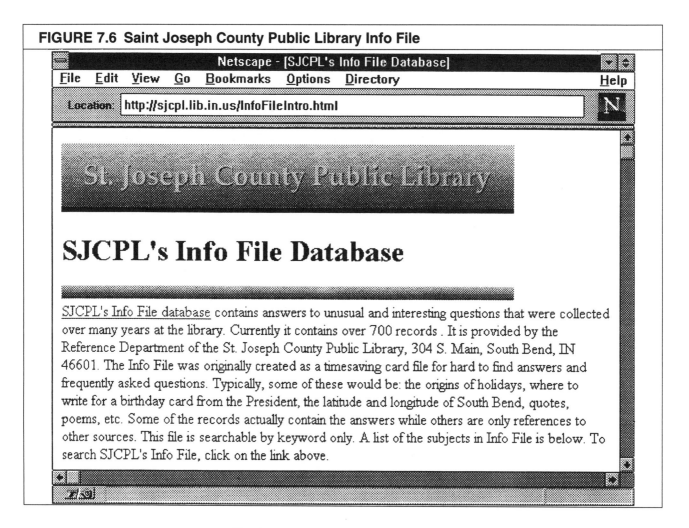

Forms

Most browsers now support forms which allow you to create an easy interface on your page to collect information from your user. The information collected is then passed onto a script for processing. The information is often search terms, which are then passed to a database server for processing

For example, the Library of Congress uses forms and scripts on their Web site to provide access to the LC Name Authorities file. Traditionally the domain of catalogers, the Name Authority file includes a wealth of information for reference librarians, helping to unravel pseudonyms and transliterations of author names.

FIGURE 7.7 Searching the Library of Congress Name Authority File

LC MUMS Z39.50 Search Form

First Record to View: Maximum Records to Retrieve:

Select Database to be Searched:

Key to Databases:

BOOKS - Books Bibliographic Records (approximately 3.8 million)
NAMES - Name Authority Records (approximately 3.4 million)

Availability: (6:30 a.m. - 9:30 p.m. Mon.-Fri.) (8 a.m. - 5 p.m. Sat.) (8 a.m. - 4:30 p.m. Sun.)

Enter Term 1:

AND OR AND NOT

Enter Term 2:

AND OR AND NOT

Enter Term 3:

For title and personal name searching only, use the Title/Personal Name form

---

Return to Z39.50 Gateway

These links between World Wide Web pages and external databases are one of the most promising developments on the Web. It's possible to develop much more sophisticated search forms through the Web than through Gopher, with the great advantage of the uniform interface of the World Wide Web browser.

Mailto Links

Mailto links are just what they sound like: links that direct mail to an e-mail address. Instead of just listing an e-mail address and expecting people to write it down and later use it in their own e-mail programs, the address can be made into an active link that will pop up a form for an e-mail message.

Mailto links have many uses. If a Web site is designed to highlight a particular product, service, or organization, it may include a mailto link for people looking for further information. There is often a Webmaster mailto link, to collect feedback on the Web site itself. Mailto links also provide an interface to other e-mail-based services, such as e-mail groups.

Many library sites use mailto links for practical purposes. The Reading (MA.) Public Library, for example, uses a mailto link on their Home Page to allow patrons to send reference questions to the library.

FIGURE 7.8 The Reading Public Library Mailto Link for Reference Questions

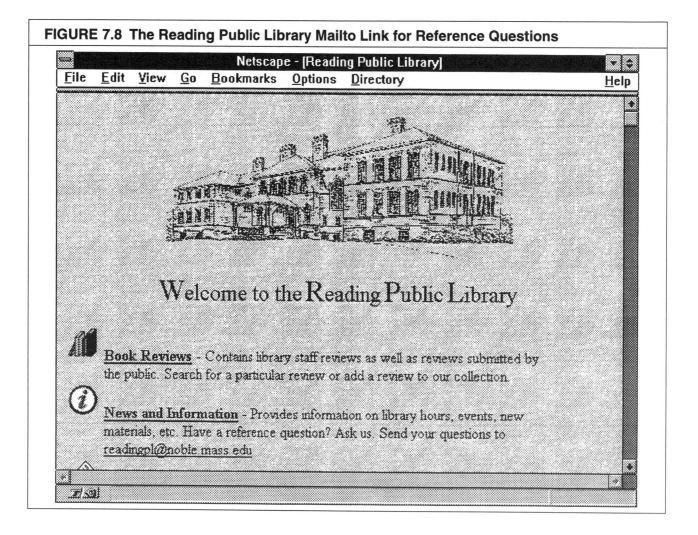

WHAT'S ON THE WEB?

The answer to this question changes every day. You will find Web sites for various branches of the government, for colleges and universities, other schools, and all types of organizations. Businesses have discovered the World Wide Web, and there are now sites for major corporations, bookstores, mail-order companies, law firms, banks, real estate companies, and many other types of businesses. The media, including newspapers, magazines, and television stations, have also been active in developing Web sites.

Many individuals now have their own home pages, either through work or school, or through their Internet Service Provider. Developing a home page is relatively easy to do, and personal home pages mark a major difference between the Web and the world of Gopher, where few individuals run their own servers. Personal home pages can highlight personal accomplishments and interests, display family photographs, and even children's art and writing.

The World Wide Web has brought major changes to the USENET newsgroups and other interest groups on the Internet, as many new sites are set up to provide access to the USENET FAQs, reading lists, and other material. These documents are far more available on the World Wide Web than they were when they were just posted to the groups and archived for FTP, and setting up a Web site provides a way to provide context and graphics.

New material is now being developed specifically for the World Wide Web, creating a new form of publishing, and a new way for all types of organizations, businesses, and private individuals to create and distribute information resources. In order to continue to provide the services that our patrons need, librarians need to understand and be a part of this new world.

SEARCHING THE WORLD WIDE WEB

As information resources proliferate on the World Wide Web, there are services that allow Web users to search the Web and find what they want. There are two basic approaches to searching the Web and other Internet resources: the subject-oriented (or hierarchical) approach, and the key word approach.

Subject-Oriented Searching

There are a number of subject-oriented guides to the World Wide Web that can help you find sites devoted to particular areas of interest. One of the best known is the Virtual Library, located at

CERN, the high energy physics research center in Switzerland; the birthplace of the World Wide Web. The Virtual Library, just as so many things on the Internet, is distributed, with parts of it existing on many different systems linked together through the Internet, rather than all being located on a single central computer. The list of subjects comes from CERN, but the individual lists are maintained by different sites around the world, mostly colleges and universities.

FIGURE 7.9 Virtual Library at CERN

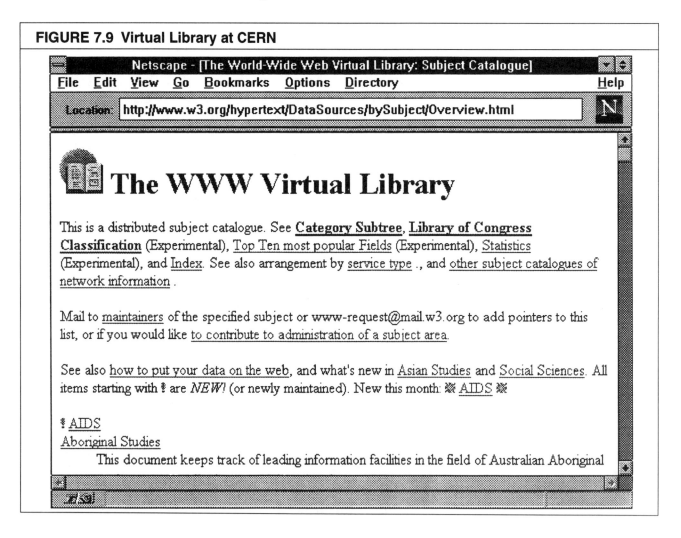

There is also a CERN list that makes an initial breakdown of subjects by Library of Congress Classification.

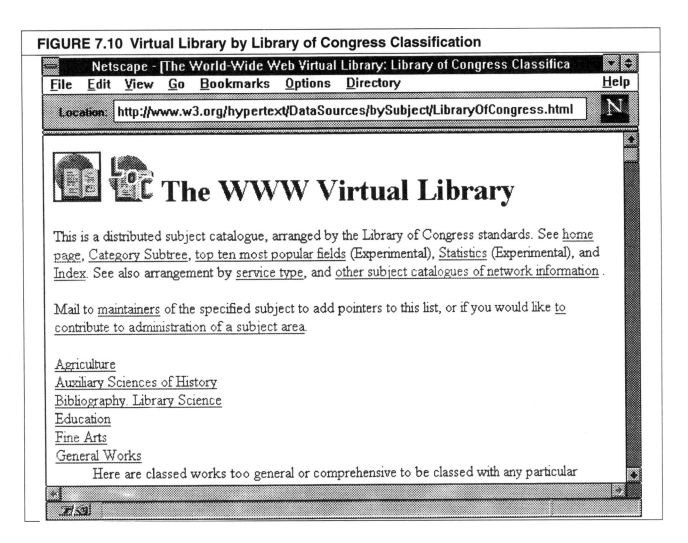

FIGURE 7.10 Virtual Library by Library of Congress Classification

One of the problems for designers of these lists is whether to have one long list of topics, for example the Civil War, Inline Skating, and Haiku, or whether to group more specific headings under more general ones, such as History, Sports, and Literature. This is a subject tree approach, where major topics branch off into narrower topics.

There are many other subject-oriented guides, with more coming all the time. These guides can save you an enormous amount of time, especially when you are looking for a variety of information rather than the answer to a single question. If you are doing a collection development project on the Civil War, going through the subject approach would give you a good idea of what's available on the Internet in this area, including an excellent Reading List from the Civil War USENET newsgroup.

Keyword Searching: Then Along Came the Spiders

The World Wide Web really is a web. Imagine a huge fish net, stretched out across the floor, with each knot representing a point, and you will see that there are an infinite number of paths to get from point A to point B. Even if A and B are adjacent to each other, you could leave one and zigzag from point to point, crossing the whole net before you reached your destination. The World Wide Web, with each link as a point, works the same way. The good thing about the web structure is that it gives you the freedom to travel in so many directions, ultimately to design your own trip. The bad thing is that it's easy to get tangled in a web.

So it was perhaps inevitable that developers would come up with an indexing scheme that would guide us through the Web, and name it after the queen of the web, the spider. There are now a number of different spiders, indexing programs which traverse the net, following link after link, gathering information about what they find and creating huge searchable databases that can help you find almost anything on the Web.

Some of the spiders running around the Internet are Lycos, WebCrawler, InfoSeek, Harvest, and (missing the analogy) the World Wide Web Worm, with more in development. Although they all operate on the same general principle, each one uses different algorithms or instructions for their travel and indexing. In addition to the true spiders, there are also indexing programs such as Aliweb, the Global Network Meta-Library, and the CUI World Wide Web Catalog which are searched in a similar fashion.

With so many different search tools, how do you know which to choose? The best way to compare these is to try the same group of searches on several different ones, and compare the results you get. Don't try to judge on the basis of a single search, and don't judge on the basis of the number of hits alone. It's a good idea to choose one system and learn as much as you can about how it works, and use that as your basic tool. By concentrating on one, you'll get to understand how it works, learn its options, and be comfortable with its commands and displays, which will increase your speed and effectiveness as a searcher.

But on occasions when you are feeling curious or desperate, you should try the others. A spider's work is never done, and you never know which spider will have made the first visit to a new site that has just what you need. Sometimes another indexing algorithm may work better in an individual case, or a smaller database may make it easier to find relevant hits than a large one.

Meet Lycos, the World's Fastest Spider

In order to give you a better idea of how spiders work, we'll use Lycos, the spider behind the world's biggest World Wide Web catalog. Lycos was developed by Dr. Michael L. Mauldin at Carnegie Mellon University, and named for the arachnid family Lycosidae, which are large ground spiders that are very quick and catch their prey by active pursuit. Lycos indexes World Wide Web servers, Gopherspace, and public FTP servers and provides an easy and flexible search interface.

Lycos is now a commercial venture, free to users and supported by advertising. The advertising appears in the form of constantly changing banners on Lycos' pages. Each banner is a link to the advertiser's Web site.

To perform a basic Lycos search you enter a few search terms and select "Search," accepting the default options for search and display. Lycos will search for entries in its catalog that have any of your search terms, or words that it considers to be related to your search term. Using an algorithm that determines the relative weight of each term on the basis of the word's "importance" and frequency, Lycos scores each hit and then displays a matching record with the highest score displayed first.

A fast, easy search engine like Lycos is even more important for librarians than for the general public. Most Internet users soon learn their way around parts of the Internet that are relevant to their personal interests, but as librarians most of us are the ultimate generalists, needing to explore every subject area on behalf of our patrons. Lycos and the other search engines and guides can help you move from subject to subject with ease.

REFERENCE WORK ON THE WORLD WIDE WEB

Unlike most Internet users, reference librarians are usually not exploring their personal interests, but looking for answers to questions posed by their patrons. Let's look at an example of how reference librarians can use Lycos to search for information on the World Wide Web.

The history and significance of the Claddagh ring is a frequent and surprisingly troublesome reference question, judging from the Stumpers archives. Here's a search on "Claddagh rings" on Lycos:

FIGURE 7.11 Lycos Search for Information on Claddagh Rings

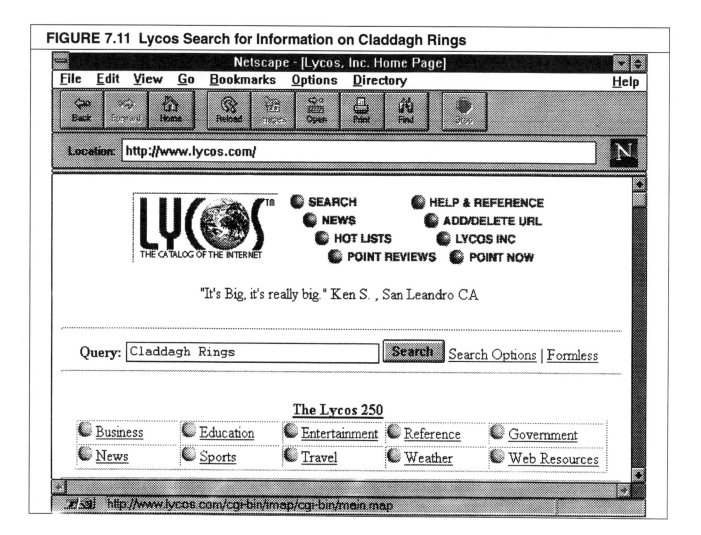

And the results:

FIGURE 7.12 Results of the Search on Claddagh Rings

- SEARCH
- NEWS
- HOT LISTS
- POINT REVIEWS
- HELP & REFERENCE
- ADD/DELETE URL
- LYCOS INC
- POINT NOW

Lycos is hiring. Examine the exciting opportunites at Lycos.
Get the facts - read the Web Catalog Size report.

Click on graphic to visit site.

Lycos search: Claddagh ring

Lycos Nov 30, 1995 catalog, 13904662 unique URLs

New Query:

Found 17837 documents matching at least one search term.
Printing only the first 10 of 16795 documents with at least scores of 0.010.

Found 674 matching words (number of documents): claddagh (154), ring (14598), rings (5558), ...

1) Claddagh Ring Prices [1.0000, 2 of 2 terms, adj 1.0]

Outline: Claddagh Ring Prices

Abstract: Prices in brackets apply to non-European Union residents 9 Carat Gold: IR&163;118.00 (IR&163;97.50) IR&163;80.00 (IR&163;66.10) IR&163;75.00 (IR&163;61.90) IR&163;42.50 (IR&163;35.10) 14 Carat Gold: IR&163;230.00 (IR&163;190.00) IR&163;168.00 (IR&163;139.00) IR&163;137.00 (IR&163;113.00) IR&163;90.00 (IR&163;74.30) 18 Carat Gold: IR&163;344.00 (IR
http://www.interact.ie/marketplace/interact/hartmann/prices.html (2k)

2) 16 - Claddagh Rings [0.9512, 2 of 2 terms, adj 1.0]

Outline: 16 - Claddagh Rings

Abstract: Claddagh Rings [Top] There are many stories about the **Claddagh ring**. **Claddagh** itself refers to a small fishing village just near Galway city. The **Claddagh ring** supposedly originated in this area. The **ring** has a design of a heart being encircled by a pair of delicate hands with a crown above the heart. In earlier times this design was the symbol of the "Fishing Kings of **Claddagh**" meaning 'in love and friendship let us reign'. In the 17th century the symbol was first depicted on a **ring** which became the fashionable exchange of friends or lovers. In marriage the

Lycos displays a generous amount of information about each hit, which gives you a good idea of which hits are going to be helpful. In this search, we see some listings for places where you can buy Claddagh rings.

As you can see, the second hit looks promising and when we connect to this page, we have just what we needed.

FIGURE 7.13 Claddagh Ring Information

Claddagh Rings

[Top]

16 - Claddagh Rings

There are many stories about the Claddagh ring. Claddagh itself refers to a small fishing village just near Galway city. The Claddagh ring supposedly originated in this area. The ring has a design of a heart being encircled by a pair of delicate hands with a crown above the heart. In earlier times this design was the symbol of the "Fishing Kings of Claddagh" meaning 'in love and friendship let us reign'. In the 17th century the symbol was first depicted on a ring which became the fashionable exchange of friends or lovers. In marriage the heart was worn towards the wrist otherwise towards the fingertips. There are many modern versions of the Claddagh Ring. Here are some folk legends about the Claddagh:

(a) Way back in the sandy mists of time, so the story went, it seemed as there was this king. This king was madly in love with a peasant woman, but as she was of a lower class the love had to go unrequited. In dread despair the king killed himself and had his hands lopped off and placed around his heart as a symbol of his undying love for the woman.

(b) It symbolizes love (heart), friendship/faith (hands) and loyalty (crown). Two hands Joined together in love and Crowned by the Glory of Christ.

(d) There was a Dublin version of this Ring that appeared some 100 years back with two hands and two Hearts but No Crown Some call this Version the Fenian Claddagh.

(e) The Crown to The Father, The Left hand to the Son, and the Right Hand the the Holy Ghost. This Explanation is directly Correlative to the Shamrock, one of the Earliest Symbols of the Holy Trinity among the Irish.

(f) Some will say Beathauile is the Crown, Anu is the Left hand, and the Dagda Mo/r is the Right hand and the Heart is the Hearts of all mankind and that which gives the everlasting music to the Gael.

(g) As legend has it, the town developed the ring (originally a sigil to be painted on ships and sails) to be worn by sailors of Claddagh. When these sailors would run into other fishermen in their waters, they would check for the sigil, and if they did not find it, they would kill them.

(h) The original Claddagh ring is generally attributed to one Richard Joyce, a native of Galway, who while being transported as a slave to the plantations of the West Indies was captured by Mediterranean pirates and sold to a Moorish goldsmith who trained him in his craft. In 1689 he was released and returned to Galway and set up his shop in the Claddagh. (The Claddagh is said to be the oldest fishing village in Ireland). By tradition the ring is taken to signify the wish that Love and Friendship should reign supreme. The hands signify friendship, the crown loyalty, and the heart love. The ring has become popular outside Connamera since the middle of the last century- its spread being helped by the vast exodus from the West during the great Famine in 1847-49. These rings were kept as heirlooms with great pride and passed from mother to daughter. Today, the ring is worn extensively across Ireland, either on the right hand with the heart turned outwards showing that the wearer is "fancy free" or with the heart turned inwards to denote that he or she is "spoken for". The pride of place is on the left hand, with the heart turned in, indicating that the wearer is happily married.

Of course, we might wonder where we happen to be getting this information. This page has a link called [Top] which moves to the home page for the Soc.Culture.Celtic FAQ:

FIGURE 7.14 Home Page of Soc.Culture.Celtic

Th Social.Culture.Celtic FAQ ▓▓▓▓▓▓▓▓▓▓▓▓▓▓▓▓▓▓▓▓▓▓▓▓▓▓▓▓▓▓▓▓▓

[Top]

The Soc.Culture.Celtic Faq

The original author of most of this fine document was the legendary *Craig Cockburn (pronounced coburn!-)* and is currently maintained by *Godfrey Nolan*, the compiler of the Irish section. If you have any comments or additions then please email me at godfrey@iol.ie

- Contributors
- Preliminary Notes

▓▓▓▓▓▓▓▓▓▓▓▓▓▓▓▓▓▓▓▓▓▓▓▓▓▓▓▓▓▓▓

Contents
- The Celts and Celtic language questions
- Alba - Scotland
- Alba Nuadh - Nova Scotia
- Breizh - Brittany
- Cymru - Wales
- Eire - Ireland
- Kernow - Cornwall
- Mannin - Isle of Man
- Celtic events & societies in major cities around the world

 To the Gaelic homepage

If we choose the link to Eire—Ireland, we see where the Claddagh Ring answer fits into this FAQ structure:

FIGURE 7.15 Eire—Ireland Page

Eire - Ireland

[Top]

Eire - Ireland

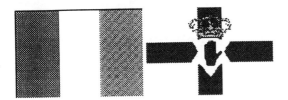

Contents

- 1 - Information from the CIA yearbook:
- 2 - What to call the Repubic and the North:
- 3 - Music & Art:
- 4 - Tourism:
- 5 - Gaeilge na hE/ireann (Irish Gaelic) Language:
- 6 - Politics:
- 7 - Sport:
- 8 - History:
- 9 - Books & Newspapers:
- 10 - Tracing Irish Ancestors:
- 11 - Internet information services:
- 12 - Mythology:
- 13 - Cuisine:
- 14 - Getting jobs in Ireland:
- 15 - Applying for Irish Citizenship:
- 16 - Claddagh Rings:
- 17 - Irish National Anthem:

To the Gaelic Homepage

The soc.culture FAQs are a great source of information about different countries, and if you explore this Ireland page a bit you will find some booklists of fiction and nonfiction related to Ireland, including a reading list on the Potato Famine, as well as a good recipe for Irish soda bread.

USING LYCOS' ADVANCED SEARCHING OPTIONS

The Claddagh ring example is an easy one because the word Claddagh is so distinctive. Lycos searches by default are Boolean OR searches, finding records that match any of your search terms. In the Claddagh ring example, Lycos actually came up with over 16,000 hits, most of them with just the word ring or rings. Because Lycos displays records a batch at a time, in order of its scoring system, those irrelevant hits didn't impede the search. You can change the default option, however, from "Find records with ANY term" to "Find records with [a certain number] of terms."

Suppose you were helping a patron who needed to check a quotation in Nathaniel Hawthorne's short story "Young Goodman Brown," and all the library copies were checked out. A Lycos search on the title finds the text of the story easily, located on a page developed by and for a college English class:

FIGURE 7.16 Young Goodman Brown Search

```
┌─────────────────────────────────────────────────────────────────────┐
│       Netscape - [Lycos search: Young Goodman Brown]          ▼ ▲    │
│ File  Edit  View  Go  Bookmarks  Options  Directory          Help   │
├─────────────────────────────────────────────────────────────────────┤
│ Lycos Nov 30, 1995 catalog, 13904662 unique URLs                    │
│                                                                      │
│                                                                      │
│                  New Query:[              ]                          │
│                                                                      │
│                                                                      │
│  Found 35329 documents matching at least one search term.           │
│  Printing only the first 10 of 13203 documents with at least scores │
│  of 0.010.                                                           │
│                                                                      │
│  Found 818 matching words (number of documents): young (29722),     │
│  goodman (2764), brown (30270), ...                                 │
│                                                                      │
│                                                                      │
│  1) Young Goodman Brown site [1.0000, 3 of 3 terms, adj 1.0]        │
│                                                                      │
│  Abstract: Young Goodman Brown This is a site exploring the short   │
│  story Young Goodman Brown , first published in 1835 by Nathaniel   │
│  Hawthorne. If you'd like, you can begin by reading the             │
│  text                                                               │
│  http://auden.fac.utexas.edu/~daniel/amlit/goodman/goodman.html (1k)│
│                                                                      │
└─────────────────────────────────────────────────────────────────────┘
```

However, we also have many irrelevant hits, such as : "Ex-Brown Bill Johnson a young man in big trouble." In this case, since my search terms only make sense in relation to each other, a better search might have been to instruct Lycos to specify a match only on all three terms.

Lycos also has options related to the display of the results list, which will either give you a more complete or briefer display for each record, and will allow you to change from the default grouping of ten records per display batch.

COLLECTION DEVELOPMENT AND READERS' ADVISORY ON THE WEB

Most of the reading lists and bibliographies available over the Internet are the product of USENET newsgroups and to a lesser extent, e-mail groups. The World Wide Web is providing a home for many of these lists, and making them easily available.

As more and more Web sites are added, additional booklists are added as people increase interesting material to attract visitors. If I developed a Web site devoted to beekeeping, for example, it would include some basic instructions for beekeepers, information on where to buy beekeeping equipment, and a booklist, to provide a way for people to get more information than it is practical to try to convey on a Web site.

A good example of this is the "Students' Reading List" and "Teachers' Reading List" of books about George Washington and the Revolution, found at the Mount Vernon site. These lists, coming from an authoritative source, could be useful for both collection development and readers' advisory work. Another example is the Knitting Page, which has a list called "Knitting References in Books." This is a collection of fiction, mostly children's books, that have something to do with wool, sheep, and knitting. This could be a good Readers' Advisory list, for example, to give to teachers planning to take children to see sheep at a farm.

One interesting reading list is associated with the Prison Awareness Project, a class offered through the Experimental College of the University of Washington and taught by prisoners at the Washington State Reformatory. Their reading list is divided into topics such as "Prisons and Prisoners," "Children and Crime," and "History of Prisons." These reading lists would be a good collection development aid in the area of criminal justice, providing a different perspective than other standard lists.

These booklists may be initially reflect the opinions of one person, the "Webmeister," but most sites collect response through mailto links, and so the lists will be challenged and developed over time, just as the USENET lists do.

FINDING THE LISTS THROUGH LYCOS

Lycos is a great way of finding reading lists, bibliographies, and resource guides on the Internet. Search and retrieval is tricky, though, because you don't know what terms the people who have created these resources have used. You might be looking for some recommended books on the martial arts, but you don't know what such lists are called. The titles could be "A Martial Arts Bibliography," "Reading List on the Martial Arts," "A List of Recommended Books on the Martial Arts," or any variation.

You could enter a search string such as MARTIAL ARTS BIBLIOGRAPHY BOOKS READING, which would certainly cover all the bases, but you would get a lot of irrelevant hits, and they might be weighted near the top, since the words Books, Bibliography, and Reading often occur together. In this instance, you have the added problem of the word Arts, which is meaningless in this search except in conjunction with Martial, and will also bring up a lot of irrelevant records.

It's easier to do this one as separate searches, matching the MARTIAL ARTS terms with each of the three "booklist" terms, BOOKS, BIBLIOGRAPHY, and READING.

If you just want to browse and see what kind of lists are out there, try doing Lycos searches on the terms ANNOTATED BIBLIOGRAPHY. Another good search for browsing is READING LISTS. If you want a real shortcut, try Bookport's site for a collection of links called "Reading Lists on the Internet." The URL for this site is http://www.bookinfo.com/Readings/ReadingsIndex.html.

LIBRARIANS AS WEB PUBLISHERS

As libraries develop their own Web sites, booklists and other guides to more traditional library services are often included. Looking at the work of other librarians is often a very useful source of ideas for collection development and Readers' Advisory work.

Librarians can also help contribute much needed content to the World Wide Web. You will find that although there are some excellent booklists out there, there are also some that need work. If you have created a book list for Readers' Advisory purposes, you can offer it as a file to a relevant World Wide Web site. It can be posted there, with your library's copyright notice, and permission to reproduce it freely but not commercially. If more librarians contribute booklists and the other types of guides that we now distribute freely on paper, there will be more resources out there for us all to share, librarians and laypeople alike!

8 LIBRARY CATALOGS, DATABASES, AND ELECTRONIC BOOKS ON THE INTERNET

The Internet opens up a whole new world for librarians and our patrons, but in many ways, you'll find electronic versions of familiar services: the card catalog, reference works, and books to go. The Internet allows you to connect to online catalogs of libraries all over the world, to databases that can provide answers to reference questions, and to electronic versions of poems, speeches, historical documents, and books.

USING LIBRARY CATALOGS ON THE INTERNET

The Internet can be a fast and easy way to connect to the online catalog of all types of libraries around the world. The ability to search other catalogs has major implications for reciprocal borrowing and interlibrary loan, of course, although sometimes the technology advances faster than does our cooperative and logistical arrangements.

The ability to search other catalogs directly benefits reference and collection development. Online catalogs offer enhanced searching capabilities not available in the traditional card catalog. The Internet gives us access to the online catalogs of major public and academic libraries, as well as specialized libraries, and there is a lot of information that can be gained from the catalog. The ability to do key word searching can help us find a title based on a few words that a patron remembers from a title or subtitle, or to combine a few elements from the author's name, the title, and the subject headings. The key word searching of summary and contents notes adds even more power, and helps make the online catalog a valuable reference tool.

For example, here is the bibliographic record for a video recording of the movie "Rear Window."

```
┌──────────────────────────────────────────────────────────────────┐
│  FIGURE 8.1  Bibliographic Record for "Rear Window"                │
├──────────────────────────────────────────────────────────────────┤
│   Title:            Rear Window                                    │
│   Imprint:          Universal City, CA : MCA Home Video, c1984.    │
│   Description:      1 videocassette (113 min.) : sd., col. ; 1/2 in.│
│   Note1:            Based on a short story by Cornell Woolrich.    │
│   Note 2:           James Stewart, Grace Kelly, Wendell Corey,     │
│                     Thelma Ritter, Raymond Burr                    │
│   Summary :         James Stewart plays a photographer with a      │
│                     broken leg, confined to his Greenwich Village  │
│                     apartment during a heat wave.  His rear window │
│                     gives him a fine view into the lives of his    │
│                     neighbors, keeping him occupied between visits │
│                     from his girlfriend, played by Grace Kelly.    │
│                     His harmless hobby of spying turns serious,    │
│                     however, when he thinks he sees a man killing  │
│                     his wife and burying her body in the flower    │
│                     garden.                                        │
│   Format:           Videocassette                                  │
│   Language :        English                                        │
│   OCLC No. :        10736088                                       │
│   Added author 1 :  Woolrich, Cornell, 1903-1968.                  │
│   Added author 2 :  Hitchcock, Alfred, 1899-                       │
│   Added author 3 :  Stewart, James, 1908-                          │
│   Added author 4 :  Grace, Princess of Monaco, 1929-1982.          │
│   Subject 1 :       Detective and mystery films.                   │
│   Subject 2 :       Feature films.                                 │
│   Dewey class :     791.43655                                      │
│   LC class :        PN1995.9D4 R4x 1984                            │
└──────────────────────────────────────────────────────────────────┘
```

The information found in this record makes it easy to combine elements to answer a number of reference questions, such as "What Alfred Hitchcock movie was based on a story by Cornell Woolrich?" or "What was the movie about a photographer with a broken leg?"

For collection development, searching the online catalogs can identify recent books on particular subjects. For example, you can search the catalogs of larger systems or systems with specialized collections to locate works on a particular subject.

USING DATABASES ON THE INTERNET

Many reference books are essentially databases published in a paper format. As many of these databases are made freely available over the Internet, librarians can save time and shelf space by learning to use the electronic versions. The electronic versions also may have additional benefits, such as more frequent updating and more flexible search strategies.

ZIP CODES

One example of how electronic versions are better is the Zip Code directories. The United States Postal Service provides easy access to their Zip Code + 4 directories. This database not only quickly returns the Zip Plus 4, it also verifies the form of address, making changes such as "St." to "Ave."

FIGURE 8.2 Zip +4, the Search

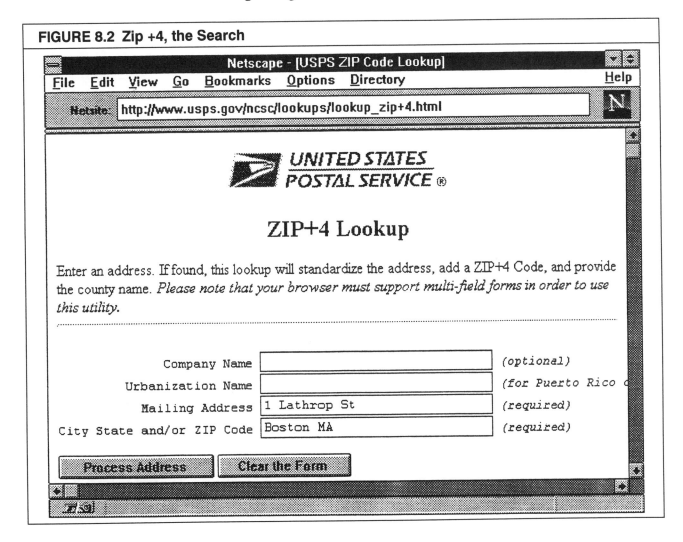

FIGURE 8.3 Zip +4, the Results

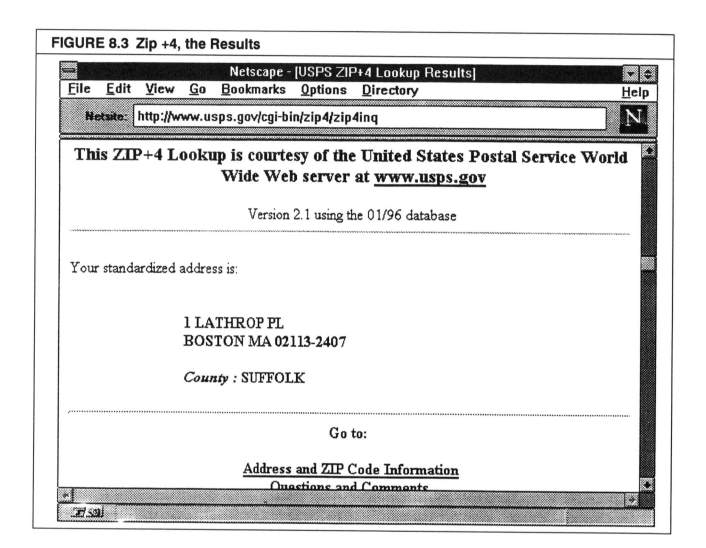

SUBWAY ROUTE FINDER

Another interesting site is the Subway Route Finder, which includes information about subway systems in New York, Paris, Tokyo, and many other cities around the world. Once you have selected a city, you enter the name of two subway stops, as seen in the following example.

FIGURE 8.4 Subway Route Finder, Search Screen

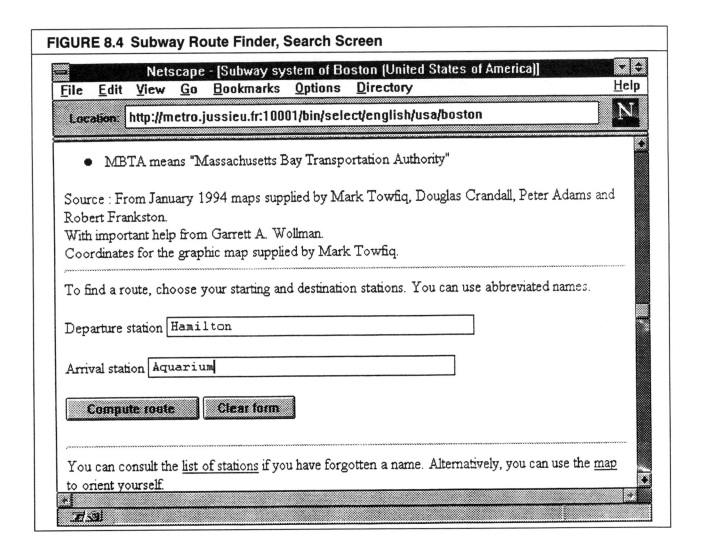

The Subway Route Finder will return the route, listing every stop along the way, including any transfer points, and estimated travel time:

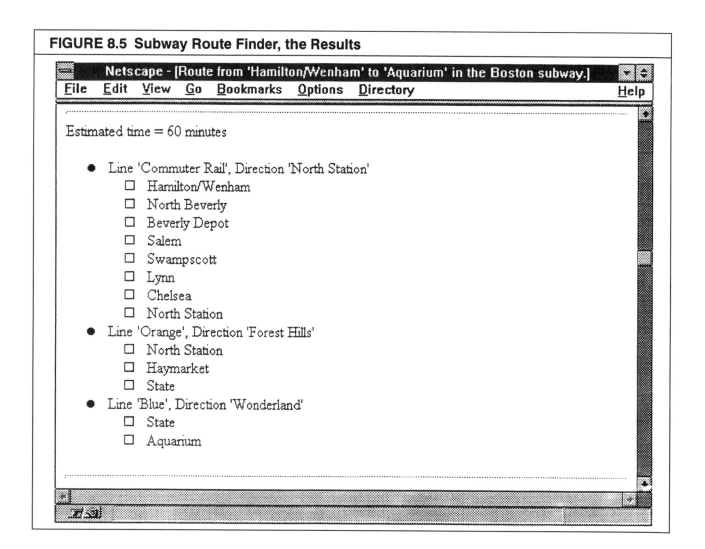

FIGURE 8.5 Subway Route Finder, the Results

UNITED STATES GAZETTEER

Looking beyond the local subway system, there is a United States Gazetteer, which allows you to look up a place name and find the location, population, etc. The Gazetteer has links to a map server and the Census statistics.

FIGURE 8.6 United States Gazetteer, the Search

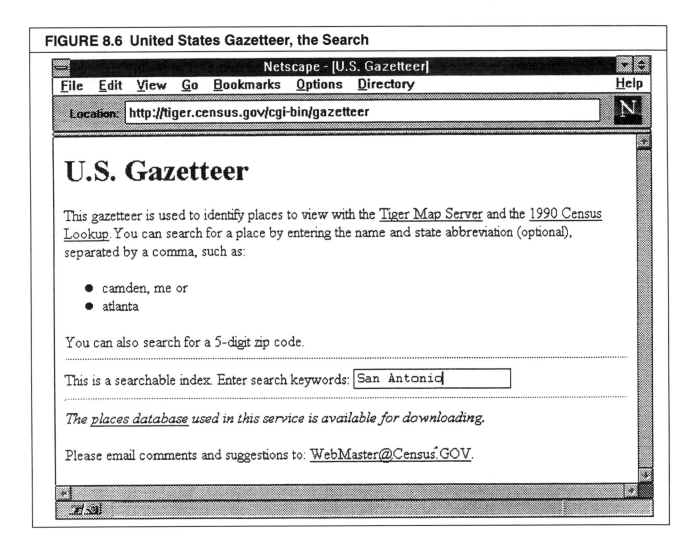

FIGURE 8.7 United States Gazetteer, the Results

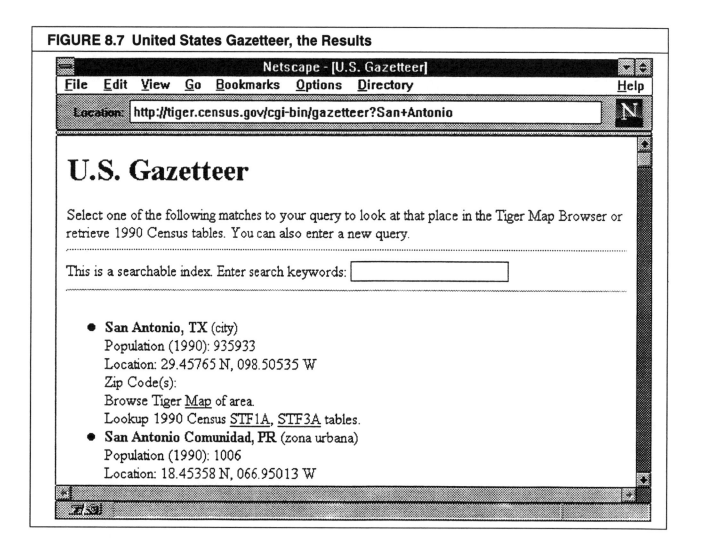

SUPREME COURT DECISIONS

All types of government information is being made available over the Internet. One important resource for reference librarians is the Supreme Court Decisions. For several years, Supreme Court decisions have been made available electronically through Project Hermes. Cornell University's Legal Information Institute provides an excellent interface to the text files, which are archived at Case Western Reserve University. The Legal Information Institute makes it easy to search the decisions through various methods, and provides a topical index to selected important pre-1990 decisions.

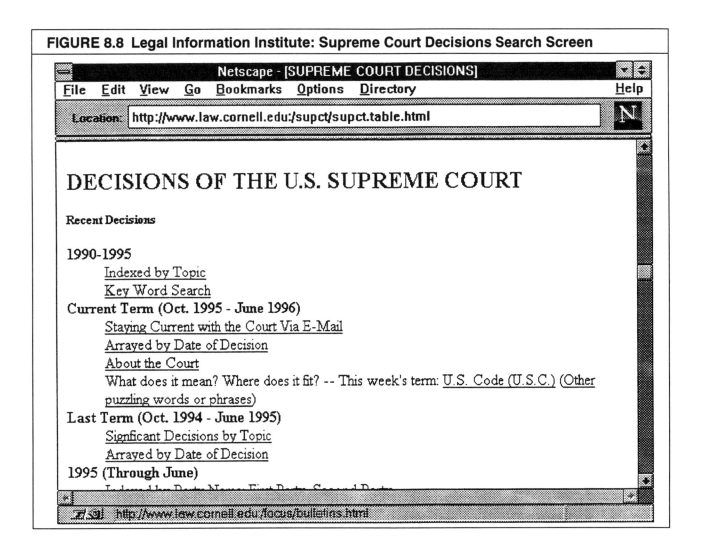

FIGURE 8.8 Legal Information Institute: Supreme Court Decisions Search Screen

This site also includes a helpful guide to the Supreme Court including a "Gallery of the Justices."

FIGURE 8.9 Legal Information Institute: The U.S. Supreme Court

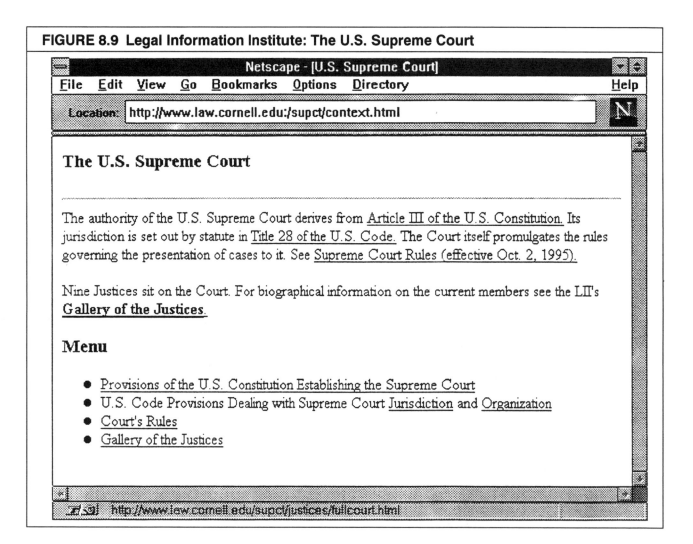

WEB-ELEMENTS

Scientific data can also be found on the Internet. One useful example is Web-Elements, an online version of the Periodic Table of Elements. The home site of the Web-Elements is the University of Sheffield in England, but there are many mirror sites at colleges and universities around the world. As Internet use has increased, the use of mirror sites has become important to help reduce the burden on a single site and to limit the distances that data needs to travel.

Here is the Web-Elements site at the University of California at Berkeley. You can get more information about an element by clicking on the chart.

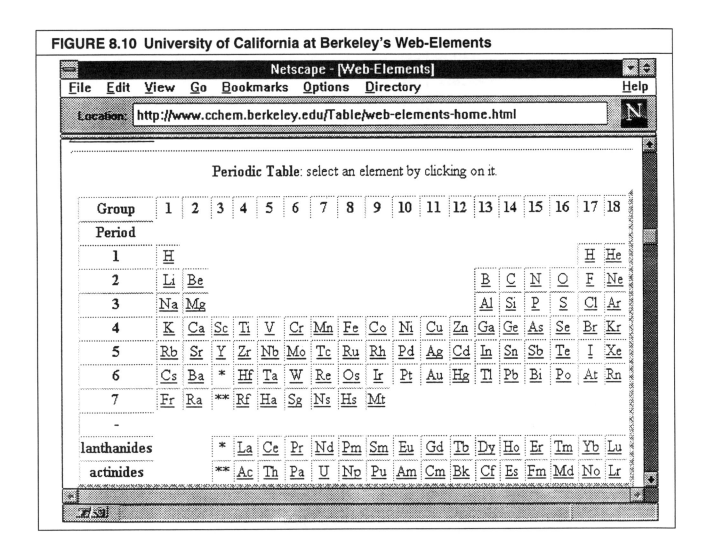

FIGURE 8.10 University of California at Berkeley's Web-Elements

USING ELECTRONIC BOOKS ON THE INTERNET

The printed word is a very convenient, inexpensive way of communicating ideas and information. A book is portable, durable, and can be used by anyone with vision, light, and literacy. However, there are some great advantages to electronic text, which can be stored and conveyed by computer, and read directly on the computer screen or printed on demand. The increasing availability of electronic text is important for both reference and collection development. Electronic text, also known as e-text, generally means electronic versions of public domain text, free of copyright restrictions and available for transfer from computer to computer.

PROJECT GUTENBERG

The standards for e-text were established by Michael Hart and Project Gutenberg. In 1971, Michael Hart was given some free time on a computer at the University of Illinois, and used it to type in "The Declaration of Independence." Hart coined the phrase "Replicator Technology" to refer to the concept that once a book or any other item is entered into a computer, it can be endlessly stored in memory, moved from computer to computer, and made available to as many people as possible.

Plain Vanilla ASCII

Project Gutenberg texts have always been made available in "Plain vanilla ASCII," meaning the low set of the American Standard Code for Information Interchange. This is a basic character set which can be read by virtually every available computer system, from old Ataris and Apple IIs to Macs, Windows PCs and Unix systems.

Because the Project Gutenberg texts can be used on any type of computer, they can be used as the basis for many types of projects. They can be converted to any format, edited to match a particular edition, annotated for a special project, or otherwise adapted for any special project.

Project Gutenberg texts have been selected to appeal to as wide a variety of potential readers as possible. They include classic works, including the plays of Shakespeare, *Moby Dick*, and *Paradise Lost*; children's books, such as *Alice in Wonderland* and *Peter Pan*, and religious works, such as the Bible and the Koran, as well as historical and public works such as the Constitution of the United States.

Project Gutenberg texts have been distributed using every service on the Internet: e-mail, USENET newsgroups, FTP, Gopher, and the World Wide Web. This reflects the easy portability of ASCII text and the general philosophy of the project: to create texts that will always be available through many generations and changes in computer systems and programs.

THE BARTLEBY LIBRARY

Project Gutenberg was the first major e-text project, but there are a number of other electronic text projects. Project Gutenberg was begun with a strong populist sense of mission, attempting to provide the widest possible distribution for as much text as possible. Volunteer labor is used, and while the editions are generally good quality, the intent was never to produce authorized or scholarly editions.

In contrast, Columbia University sponsors the Bartleby Library, named after the main character in Herman Melville's story, "Bartleby the Scrivener." A scrivener's job was to make careful, accurate copies of important documents, and that's what Columbia University is doing with this project, which has made available hypertext versions of a number of works of interest to librarians.

FIGURE 8.11 Columbia University's Bartleby Library

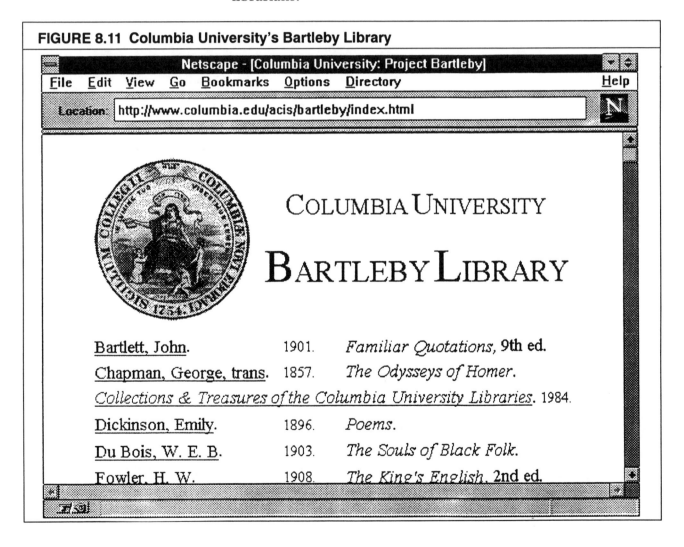

Each work is carefully selected, meticulously transcribed, and given a complete bibliographic citation. One selection that is especially useful for reference is "Inaugural Addresses of the Presidents." Every library should be able to provide this type of material, but how often do patrons really request the Inaugural Address of Martin Van Buren? Selective use of electronic works for important but less frequently needed material reflects the move in collection development from emphasis on ownership to access, and from "just-in-case" purchases to "just-in-time" document delivery.

FIGURE 8.12 Inaugural Addresses of the Presidents

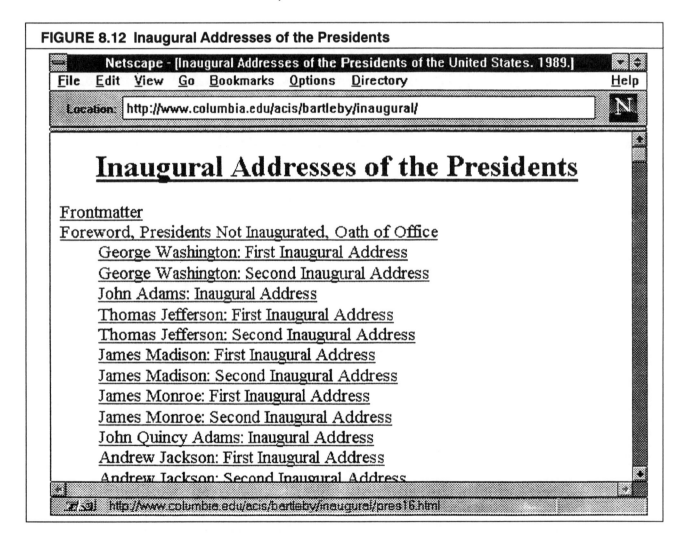

OTHER PROJECTS

There are also a number of smaller projects, many as part of World Wide Web pages devoted to particular people, places, and subject areas. Some writers are now publishing their own works on the Internet, and publishers are beginning to offer sample chapters of new books at their own sites. Sample chapters and excerpts offer librarians a great "sneak preview" of possible purchases.

One interesting use of e-text is to make available oral history material. An example of this is the collection of Hiroshima Survivors stories that are part of the Online Book Initiative of Software Tool and Die's public access system, known as the World.

USES FOR E-TEXT

When the topic of electronic text comes up, the usual reaction is to wonder who would want to curl up in bed with a computer instead of a good book, or try to read electronic text on the beach or in the bathtub. But while books have many advantages for pleasure reading, there are many special uses for electronic texts.

Although longer works may be expensive and inconvenient to print on demand or read from a screen, short, separate pieces of text like speeches, historical documents, stories, and poems work particularly well as e-text, since they are easy to download and print on demand, or to send to a patron via e-mail.

One of the greatest benefits of electronic text is that it is searchable. E-text can be searched on the Internet, using any search facility built into an Internet client such as a Web browser, or downloaded to a word processing program and searched there. The searchability can make it easy to find an obscure quotation in Shakespeare, the Bible, or any other available work. Because you have the entire work, you can not only find a quotation, but see it in context and print out the whole relevant section, if needed.

Here's the Shakespeare home page, a special project by Jeremy Hylton of The Tech, a newspaper at the Massachusetts Institute of Technology. The complete works of Shakespeare are available here, with a search engine that can search the entire collection or selected works. Here's a search on the terms Rosemary and Remembrance, and the results. Note the link from the quote to the full text of the play.

FIGURE 8.13 Shakespeare Search

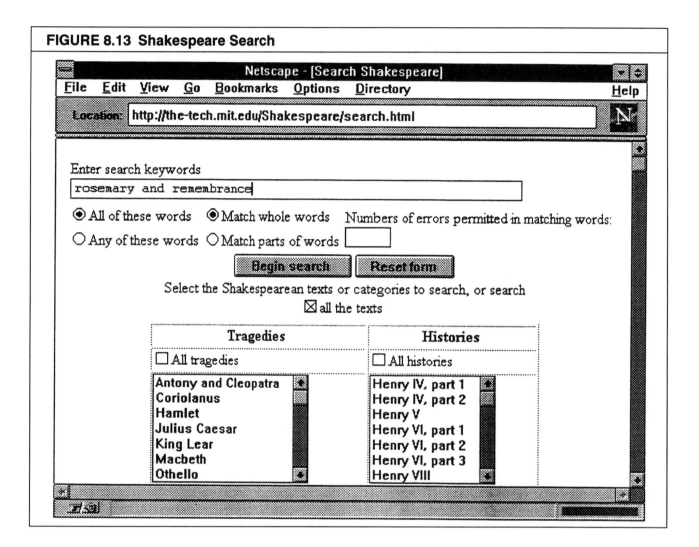

FIGURE 8.14 Shakespeare Search Results

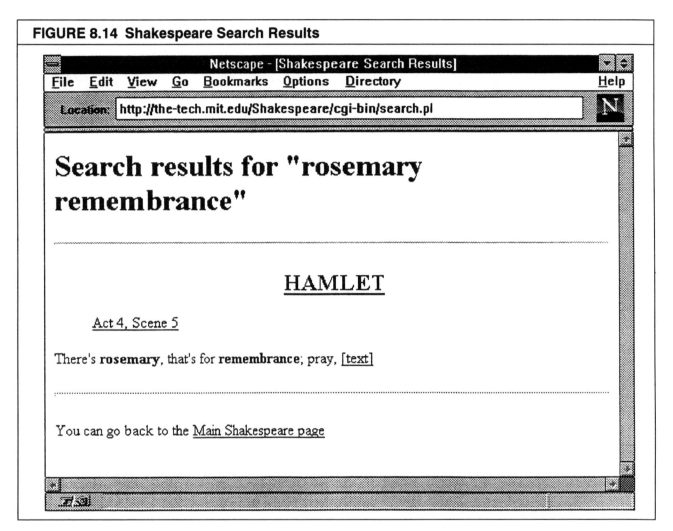

Another Webmaster at The Tech, Daniel Stevenson, has an extremely useful site, with the English translations of over 300 Greek and Roman classics.

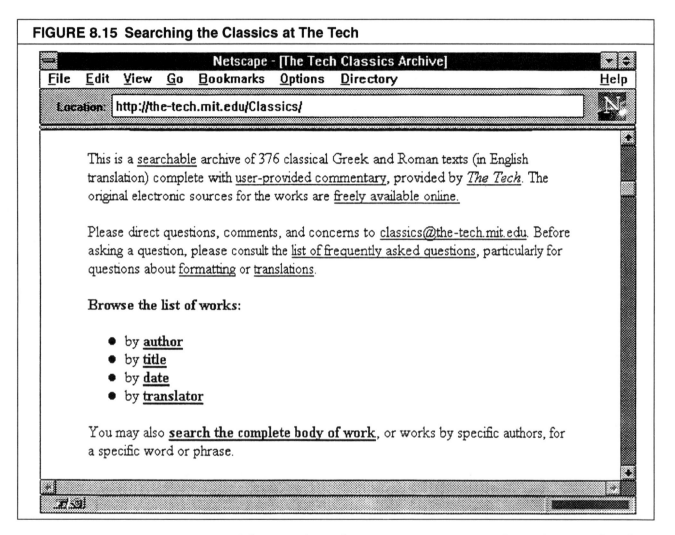

FIGURE 8.15 Searching the Classics at The Tech

These and similar sites are important for reference, for their searchability, and collection development, for their ability to deliver full text of important, but infrequently requested works. A small branch library with Internet access can have the complete works of all these classic works available at all times, without using up limited shelf space.

E-text is also of great benefit to teachers. High school teachers, for example, can download a work like *Beowulf* at the library, and use it in their own word processing program. This not only gives them a searchable version, but the ability to produce their own annotated teaching editions, which can be updated and developed over time. Students can also benefit from downloaded text, using it, for example, to find quotations and move them directly into research papers. This same idea, of course, works well for all types of writers and researchers.

Another advantage of downloaded text is the ability to use a word processing or desktop publishing program to produce and print a copy of a psalm or poem or other document that looks a lot better than a photocopy from a book. Student artists may download a copy of a poem, fairy tale or fable, and produce their own illustrated version.

There are also times when a patron might prefer a book, but all copies are out. This is especially a problem with books assigned in school, despite our best efforts. A student who needs to read three chapters for the next day might prefer the text as a print out or on a diskette rather than not have access to it at all.

LIBRARIANS AND ELECTRONIC TEXT

Librarians work with material in a number of formats; books, periodicals, sound recordings, video recordings, CD-ROM, and much more, all of which have their own advantages and disadvantages, and we need to include electronic resources, including electronic texts, as part of the mix.

Because the public generally may not be familiar with e-text alternatives, we may need to be proactive in these services. Far more schools, for example, have access to PCs than have Internet access, and librarians can offer to download text to diskettes for teachers, students, and others. Libraries may want to download certain basic collections of text and keep them on diskettes or mounted on the hard drives of public access PCs. This is also a way to give offline branches and book mobiles the benefits of electronic text.

BRAVE NEW WORLD?

For many librarians, the move to electronic catalogs, electronic databases, and electronic books can seem threatening. We are being given so many new things to learn, in a rapidly changing environment, and yet demand for traditional services continues as well.

But the things that we are doing with the new electronic media are not new, they are the same basic services that we have always provided, just delivered in new ways. We are still trying to find the information that our patrons want, and to organize and arrange that information in a logical and orderly manner. Ranganathan's First Law of Library Science, "Save the Time of the Reader," applies to the design of our World Wide Web sites as well as the layout of our library building. We are saving the time of the reader when we can print out a copy of one of the lesser known plays by Aristophanes rather than waiting to get it on Interlibrary Loan, and when we can use key word searching to find a quotation from Shakespeare that wasn't familiar enough to make Bartlett's.

In a world with a proliferation of information in all formats, we need skilled and dedicated librarians more than ever to guide our users through the maze and help them find the resources they want and need.

APPENDIX I
THE VIRTUAL VERTICAL FILE

Libraries have traditionally used the vertical file to hold pamphlets, flyers, and clippings that are useful for reference. Much of this material is provided free or for a nominal cost by various non-profit organizations who have education and outreach as part of their mission. This includes valuable health information and statistics from associations designed to promote awareness and support research of a particular disease or health issue, career information from professional organizations, information on environmental issues from Greenpeace and the Sierra Club, etc. It also includes information provided free as a public service or public relations tool by businesses, and information on a variety of topics from different departments and agencies of federal, state, and local government.

This same type of information is now freely being made available over the Internet. The publishers of this information are private and public organizations of all types, from giant corporations to local fan clubs, and individuals with a special interest in a topic. As in any type of reference work, it's not always easy to find the information you need, or to evaluate the currency and accuracy of the information that you find. However, time and experience are the best way to develop skills in both searching and evaluation.

The following list of resources in intended to highlight some sites that should have helpful information for reference librarians. The resources here were selected on the basis of content, and organization and presentation of information. Although many of these sites include excellent graphics, unless otherwise noted, all work well for text-based browsers such as Lynx. The list is selective and representative, not comprehensive, but rather should serve as a starting point for a reference tour of the Internet.

ADOPTION

AdoptioNetwork is a site with links to serve all people involved in the adoption process: adoptive parents, birthparents, and adopted children. The links include helpful articles as well as referral information, statistics, and links to other sites. This site is highly recommended as a starting point for any adoption issue.

URL: http://www.infi.net/adopt

AFRICAN-AMERICANS

There are many good starting points for African-American information on the Internet. One recommended site is DRUM, with links to information on the arts, history, and many social and cultural issues.

> URL: http://drum.ncsc.org/

An excellent, established list of resources of interest to African Americans is "Black/African Related Resources" maintained by Art McGee at the University of Pennsylvania, and often referred to as "Art McGee's List."

> URL: http://www.sas.upenn.edu/African_Studies/
> Home_Page/mcgee.html

ALCOHOL, DRUG, AND OTHER ADDICTION RESOURES

There are many addiction-related resources on the World Wide Web. Some are the official sites for Alcoholics Anonymous and other addiction-related support groups, while others are sponsored by treatment centers.

The Web of Addictions is a general, informational site with ties to no particular organization but links to many. This site, maintained by Andrew L. Homer, Ph.D. and Dick Dillon, is an attempt to provide access to accurate information on a variety of addiction-related issues.

> URL: http://www.well.com/user/woa/

ANIMAL RIGHTS AND VEGETARIANISM

Animal Rights Resource Site

This site, maintained by Ben Leamy and Donald Graft, is a collection of links to a variety of resources related to all aspects of animal rights and vegetarian/vegan issues. This includes essays, FAQs, collections of quotations and poems, and links to other organizations and resources, on and off the Internet.

> URL: http://envirolink.org/arrs/

Rec.food.vegetarian World Guide to Vegetarianism

This is a series of twenty files that are an online directory of information about vegetarian and vegetarian-friendly restaurants all over the world, plus information on vegetarian meals on airlines, cruise ships, and railroads, and vegetarian resources on the Internet.

> URL: //www.cis.ohio-state.edu/hypertext/faq/usenet/
> vegetarian/guide/top.html

ANIMALS

NetVet is a service of the Washington University Division of Comparative Medicine, and provides access to a variety of veterinary and general animal-related resources. For reference, the most useful link is probably The Electronic Zoo, a collection of links to all types of resources related to animals, both domestic (dogs, cats, horses) and wild (marine mammals, amphibians, reptiles, etc.) The resources here include FAQs from USENET newsgroups and other pages and projects. Whether you are looking for information on beagle breeders or online frog dissection, the Electronic Zoo is a good place to start.

URL: http://netvet.wustl.edu/vet.htm

ENGLISH USAGE

Alt.usage.english FAQ

"The Alt.usage.english FAQ File" by Mark Israel is a great reference help for any question on grammar or style. It also includes information on the origin of many words and phrases, including some that come up often on Stumpers and in our libraries such as posh, OK, SOS, blue moon, and whole nine yards. These all have multiple theories of origin, and the answers here are a good roundup of the major theories, with citations to various books.

There is also information here on spoonerisms, Tom Swifties, the proper names for some punctuation marks (@, for example, the "commercial at sign"), and words that are their own antonyms.

There are many references here to recommended books and Internet sources, making this a great reference tool for many common questions.

URL: http://www.cis.ohio-state.edu/hypertext/faq/usenet/
alt-usage-english-faq/faq.html

OWL: The Online Writer's Laboratory (Purdue University)

Several colleges and universities have online writer's resources, but Purdue's is exceptional. It includes the text of many handouts on grammar, parts of speech, spelling, and much more. For some subjects, there is a set of handouts: an information file, a set of exercises, and a set of answers and explanations. The handouts are specific and detailed, and the site is unusually well-organized, with three separte listings of files (by name, by subject, and in an outline format).

In addition to these basic handouts, there are also excellent guides to outlining, writing, revision, and proofreading research papers, including one on "Quoting, Paraphrasing, and Summarizing," and one on "Coping with Writer's Anxiety." There is also a section devoted to résumés and related writing, including cover letters and acceptance letters.

As well, there are links to related Internet resources. This site was designed to support the needs of college students, but it has information that should help anyone seeking to improve their writing skills.

URL: http://owl.trc.purdue.edu

GARDENS AND GARDENING

GardenNet is an excellent site for gardening information, including online ordering of catalogs. One section reference librarians should note is the Guide to Gardens of the USA, an extensive listing of public gardens by state and by type, including fragrance gardens, Shakespearean gardens, children's gardens, and gardens with full wheelchair access.

URL: http://www.olympus.net/gardens/welcome.htm

GENEALOGY

Genealogical information abounds on the Internet, but the Genealogy Home Page is a great starting point and guide to various important genealogical resources. Here you will find links to the FAQ files and other resources created by the e-mail group ROOTS-L and the various USENET newsgroups in the soc.genealogy hierarchy, which includes separate groups and FAQs for different areas of genealogy, including Jewish, British, and Irish, Australian, and New Zealandish, Medieval, and much more. The FAQs for these groups have many addresses and other pointers to information.

Many genealogists are publishing and updating their research on the Internet, and you will also find pointers to the many page devoted to various family projects. One interesting resource is the ROOTS Surname List Name Finder. This is a database consisting of over 80,000 surnames submitted by over 5,000 genealogists. If you have a patron who is working on a genealogical project, you can use this database to put him or her in touch with others who may have helpful information to share, which could save both researchers many hours of duplicated labor.

The Genealogy Home Page is maintained by Stephen A. Wood.

URL: http://ftp.cac.psu.edu/~saw/genealogy.html

HEALTH

Heart Disease

The American Heart Association's World Wide Web site includes biostatistical fact sheets on the incidence of cardiovascular disease in different ethnic groups and people with various risk factors. There is also a "Heart and Stroke Guide" with over 200 files on various topics.

http://www.amhrt.org/resources.html

Alzheimer's Association

The Alzheimer's Association home page includes substantial information about this disease, including information for caregivers, reading lists, and medical information.

URL: http://www.alz.org/

Online Birth Center

The Online Birth Center is a collection of links to information about midwifery, pregnancy, childbirth, and breastfeeding, with links to some general parenting and child health resources as well. Some of the information that you will find here includes the sci.med.midwifery FAQs, and information on nutrition and pregnancy, family planning, infertility, home birth, and much more.

URL: http://www.efn.org/~djz/birth/birthindex.html

CancerNet

CancerNet provides current, authoritative information from the National Cancer Institute. This includes summaries from the PDQ database for doctors and patients on the diagnosis, staging, and treatment and many different types of cancer.

URL: http://wwwicic.nci.nih.gov/CancerNet.html

OncoLink

OncoLink has a much broader range of information for cancer patients and their families, including Cancer FAQ files from different groups, information on financial and insurance issues for patients, group support and personal experiences, and links to other Internet resources related to cancer, including the many sites each devoted to a single type of cancer.

URL: http://oncolink.upenn.edu/

Asthma

The FAQs from alt.support.asthma include all kinds of useful information for asthma patients.

URL: http://www.cco.caltech.edu/~wrean/asthma-gen.html

Fibromyalgia Information

This site includes a great deal of useful information about this common but misunderstood condition, including FAQs for patients and doctors and a FAQ on pain.

URL: http://metro.turnpike.net/C/cfs-news/fibro.html

Chronic Fatigue Syndrome/Myalgic Encephalomyelitis

This is an extensive, well-organized site maintained by Roger Burns. There is much useful information here including FAQs, and an electronic resource guide and links to other pages.

URL: http://metro.turnpike.net/C/cfs-news/

CDC Diabetes Home Page

The CDC Diabetes Home Page is a project of the Division of Diabetes Translation, of the National Center for Chronic Disease Prevention, and Health Promotion of the Centers for Disease Control and Prevention. The site includes fact sheets on the different types of diabetes, the incidence of diabetes among different population groups, treatment options, and more. The site also solicits questions by e-mail with answers posted on the page.

URL: http://www.cdc.gov/nccdphp/ddt/ddthome.htm

Parkinson's Disease Web

This is an exemplary medical site, created by Project Coordinator Ken Bernstein and a distinguished medical and editorial panel. This site includes well-organized, high quality information on the causes, symptoms, and medical, surgical, and behavioral treatment of Parkinson's Disease.

URL: http://neuro-chief-e.mgh.harvard.edu/
parkinsonsweb/Main/pdmain.html

LAW AND GOVERNMENT

FedWorld

The United States government is one of the world's greatest purveyors of information, on paper and now on the World Wide Web. FedWorld provides organized links to much of the information made available by various agencies and departments of the federal government.

URL: http://www.fedworld.gov

Thomas

Thomas, "in the spirit of Thomas Jefferson," is one of the most important reference sites on the Internet. Updated several times a day, Thomas provides the full text of all versions of House and Senate bills, searchable by key word or bill number, as well as the full text of the Congressional Record.

URL: //http://thomas.loc.gov

Project Vote Smart

Project Vote Smart is a meticulously researched, organized, and maintained site, dedicated to providing Americans with accurate, unbiased information about our elected officials and political candidates. This includes biographical information, voting records, responses to Project Vote Smarts surveys, and much more.

In addition to information about candidates and office holders, there is a great state-by-state section, with links to online versions of state constitutions, legislative directories, etc. There are also some general resources on how our government works, and, in case you can't find what you need, a toll free phone number for help.

URL: http://www.vote-smart.org

Individual Rights in America: A Citizen's Guide to Internet Resources

This is an exceptional site for information on anything related to the rights of American citizens. The main menu is organized according to the general source of rights, for example, "Rights under the Constitution and Bill of Rights," "Rights under Select Federal Statutes," etc., but an alternative "Detailed Table of Contents" makes it easy to locate any particular area of interest. Also handy is a separate menu providing quick access to the text of all documents included at this site, and there are many, from the Constitution and Bill of Rights to the Americans with Disabilities Act and the Fair Credit Reporting Act to the Library Bill of Rights and even historical works such as Thoreau essay "On Civil Disobedience."

This comprehensive and well-organized site is maintained by Michele Pfaff and David Bachman and is a great starting point for any question related to the rights of citizens.

URL: http://www.lib.umich.edu/chdocs/rights/Citizen.html

Copyright

Marvel, the Library of Congress Gopher, provides basic information on various aspects of copyright.

URL: gopher://marvel.loc.gov/11/copyright

For a different perspective, there's an excellent, multi-part Copyright FAQ that is especially helpful for copyright issues arising from the Internet and other computer and software issues.
http://www.cis.ohio-state.edu/hypertext/faq/usenet/Copyright-FAQ/top.html

MUSIC

Cyberverse Music Library

This site provides resource guides for Music Education, Ethnomusicology, Music History, Music Theory, Music Therapy, Composers, Instruments, and more. This is a well-organized and well-maintained site and a great starting point for music information.
http://cedar.evansville.edu/~cf4/mlib/mlib.shtml

Opera Stories and Background

This resource, part BMG Music's web site, is a listing of many popular operas. Each entry includes basic information (the composer, librettist, date, etc.) and an act by act summary of the opera. There are even sound clips of each major aria.
URL: http://classicalmus.com/bmgclassics/opera/index.html

The Piano Page

This is the home page for the Piano Technician's Guild, and includes a great deal of useful information on the care and maintenance of pianos.
http://www.prairienet.org/arts/ptg/homepage.html

BluesNet, the Internet Blues Resource

This is a great site for information about the Blues. One unusual feature is a long list of "mentors." Each mentor is an expert on a particular artist or aspect of the Blues, and is willing to answer questions by e-mail.
http://dragon.acadiau.ca/~rob/blues/blues.htm

NOBEL PRIZES

The Nobel Foundation has a great site, which includes general information on the foundations and the awards. The most useful thing here, however, is the searchable Directory of Laureates. You can search the Directory in many ways, specifying prize categories (Physics, Literature, Peace, etc.); the year(s) of awards; name, country, or university; years of birth and/or death; or even words in the citation for a Laureate.
URL: http://www.nobel.se/

RELIGION

The WWW Bible Gateway

The WWW Bible Gateway, a service of Gospel Communications, is a very handy site for reference. The search options allow you to choose from a number of different versions of the Bible, and then either enter a passage, for example, "Psalms 23:1" or key word search terms, such as "Bildad the Shuhite" or "Plowshares Swords."

The WWW Bible Gateway gives every library quick, searchable access to several versions of the Bible. There are also options to change the language of both the search screens and text searched.

http://www.gospelcom.net/bible

Institute for Christian Leadership

The Institute of Christian Leadership provides resources to the Christian higher education community. The ICL Web site is a well-organized site with links to its own material and a variety of sites elsewhere on the Internet. One of the best known resources here is the "Guide to Christian Resources on the Internet," also known as "Not Just Bibles."

There's also an online guide to Christian literature on the Internet, which is divided into sections including Bibles, Books, Articles, Sermons, and Creeds and Confessions.

URL: http:\\www.iclnet.org

Catholic Information on the Internet

The Vatican's Path to Freedom Foundation sposors this official World Wide Web site for the Catholic Church. The mission of this site is to provide an authoritative source of information for the Catholic community as well as for members of academia and the media. There is some useful, well-organized information at this site, as well as links to resources elsewhere on the Internet. This is an especially good source of information on the Pope's writings, speeches, and travels.

URL: //www.catholic.net

Shamash: The Jewish Internet Consortium

There's a lot of information here, and connections to various Jewish organizations around the world. For reference, the most useful resource is probably the FAQ files for soc.culture.jewish. These files are designed to be used in conjunction with the group's Judaism Reading Lists, also maintained by Daniel J. Faigin. The FAQ is a basic overview of Jewish beliefs and practices, with special attention to holidays, Kosher law and practice, clothing, and customs.

URL: http://shamash.org

SPORTS

Starting Point provides links to all types of sports information, from the official sites for different leagues and teams and fan pages for different players, as well as information pages for sports' participants.

URL: http://www.stpt.com/sports.html

SCIENCE

The Nine Planets: A Multimedia Tour of the Solar System

There are beautiful graphics here, as well as sound files, but you really need to see this site through Lynx to appreciate how much information is here and how well-presented it is. There's information here about every planet as well as every moon of every planet. Don't miss the Appendices, which have a lot of reference potential. There's a section on the chronology of solar system discovery, information on the biggest planets and moons and other solar system superlatives, and a section on hypothetical planets and moons—ones that were "discovered" at some point but whose existence was never verified.

URL: http://seds.lpl.arizona.edu/nineplanets/nineplanets/
nineplanets.html

VolcanoWorld

VolcanoWorld, located at the University of North Dakota, is an educational project with a distinguished development team, designed to bring current, accurate information on volcano activity, past and present, to selected target groups, including students and visitors to National Parks, as well as the general public.

VolcanoWorld's Web site has lots of information that would be great for homework help. There are lists and charts of volcanos of the world, with statistics on the deadliest eruptions, etc.

URL: http://volcano.und.nodak.edu

EcoNet

EcoNet provides information on environmental news, organizations, and conferences, as well as an extensive set of resources on various environmental issues, including acid rain, biodiversity, sustainable development, and climate issues, including ozone depletion.

http://www.econet.apc.org/econet/

APPENDIX II
THE LIST OF LISTS

The Bible says, "of books and the making of books, there is no end." It would seem just as true that "of books and the *listing* of books, there is no end." People love to make lists of the best books, and the Internet has provided a new way for people to share these lists. Booklists are created for the USENET newsgroups and e-mail groups, and many of these can be found on their own home pages or at various archive sites. Other booklists are created especially for subject-oriented sites, or are made available publicly as part of the educational outreach mission of an organization.

Booklists on the Internet vary greatly in style, format, and quality. Some are the professional projects of librarians and scholars, while others are labors of love, but all can be useful for librarians who are involved in collection development and readers' advisory work. Some of the booklists found on the Internet can also provide a quick start for students beginning research projects, or as a source of ideas for librarians planning book talks, displays, or booklists of their own.

The following list of lists is a selection of representative, useful booklists of various kinds found on the Internet. They were selected to reflect the diversity of booklisting activity on the Internet, from scholarly projects to personal labors of love. The level of bibliographic citation, highly variable on the Internet, was not a prime consideration.

In all cases, these are available on the World Wide Web using the URL that I have included. Many, especially those associated with a USENET newsgroup, can also be retrieved by anonymous FTP or mail-server. Many are found on more than one site, and all addresses are subject to change.

RECOMMENDED BOOKS, BESTSELLERS, AND BOOK AWARDS

The following sites are useful for booklists that cross subject lines.

Scholar's Booklink

Many publishers on the Internet are now offering tables of contents, excerpts, and even whole sample chapters for some of their new books, and new books are also being reviewed in online journals. Scholar's Booklink, a service of the Todd Library, Middle Tennessee State University, provides organized access to this information for selected books of academic interest.

Scholar's Booklink is divided into eight major general subject areas, including Art and Music, Literature and Theatre, and Business and Economics. Each division includes a list of citations for the books selected, including a link to the reviews or excerpts at other sites.

This is a well-organized, useful service. Although there aren't many titles at this writing, there are some interesting things here, including a link to the American Journal of Nursing's Best Books of the Year. This project, the work of Ken Middleton, is definitely a project with potential for collection development, and a site to watch.

URL: http://www.mtsu.edu/mtsu/library/bklink/
bklink.html

Publishers Weekly Bestseller Lists

The Publishers Weekly bestseller lists are available through the Bookwire, a World Wide Web page full of great book-related information. All the Publishers Weekly lists are here: Hardcover Fiction, Hardcover Nonfiction, Mass Market Paperback, Trade Paperback, Children's, Religion, Computer, Audio Fiction, and Audio Nonfiction. For many of the titles, the list includes links to information about the book and author from the publisher's Web site.

URL: http://www.bookwire.com/pw/bsl/bestseller-
index.html

Best-seller Lists from USA Today

USA Today has the list of the current bestselling 150 books available at their site. This is an interesting contrast to the Publishers Weekly lists, because it includes all types of books, hardcover and paperback, adult and children's, in order of their sales figures. The Books section also includes many other interesting features of interest to librarians, including the full text of many recent articles about books and authors.

URL: http://www.usatoday.com:80/life/enter/books/
leb.htm

Book Awards from Bookwire

Bookwire posts news about current book awards and nominations, and provides an index to sites with information about dozens of different book awards for all genres and many different countries.

URL: http://www.bookwire.com/awards/

ANIMALS AND PETS

Dogs: Publications

The work of Cindy Tittle Moore, this is a comprehensive, annotated guide to the best books in all areas of dog care, breeding, and training.

> URL: http://www.zmall.com/pet_talk/tittle/pets/dog-faqs/
> publications.html

Books about Llamas

This booklist, selected by Karen Conyngham, is part of the LlamaWeb Home Page, and includes books on all aspects of llamas, including health care, training, packing, spinning, and investing.

> URL: http://www.webcom.com/~degraham/Assn/
> BksAdult.html

Raptors: Reference List

An extensive, well-organinzed, annotated list of books, videos, and curriculum resources related to the study and preservation of hawks, eagles, and other birds of prey, maintained by The Raptor Center as part of their Web site.

> URL: http://www.raptor.cvm.umn.edu/raptor/
> booklist.html

Sea World/Busch Gardens

The SeaWorld/Busch Gardens site has an "Animal Information" section that lists many types of animals, including Baleen Whales, Bottlenose Dolphins, and Gorillas, as well as subjects such as Biodiversity. Choosing any of these topics will get you to a list of subtopics, including bibliographies and books for young readers.

> URL: http://www.bev.net/education/SeaWorld/

CAREERS AND PERSONAL FINANCE

Career Action Center—Recommended Reading on Select Topics

This is an excellent, comprehensive, and well-organized guide to books on career development, including a section devoted to "Electronic Work Search Books."

> URL: http://www.gatenet.com/cac/readlist.html

Homebuyers' Fair Recommended Reading

A concise but useful guide to the most useful books on buying a home.

    URL: http://www.homefair.com/homefair/reading.html

COMPUTER SCIENCE AND TECHNOLOGY

Recommended Cyberpunk Reading List

Bruce Sterling's list of the Canon of Cyberpunk, including fiction, nonfiction and magazines.

    URL: gopher://gopher.well.sf.ca.us/00/Publications/
        authors/Sterling/cyberpunk_library.txt

A Concise Guide to UNIX Books

This well-known, annotated list of Unix books is maintained by Samuel Ko.

    http: //www.cis.ohio-state.edu/hypertext/faq/usenet/
        books/unix/faq.html

Reading List on Parallel Programming Languages

Guy E. Blelloch maintains an extensive, well-organized list of references to various classes of parallel programming languages, with pointers to other sites.

    URL: http://www.cs.cmu.edu/Web/Groups/scandal/www/
        parallel-lang.html

The Programmers' Booklist

This booklist was originally created by Sunir Shah to help programmers select and order technical books that were not carried by general bookstores. It includes over 400 books divided into topics such as Networks, Object Oriented Programming, Visual Basic, Compilers, and Algorithms. It also includes entries for Magazines, FTP Sites, and World Wide Web pages. It is well-organized and frequently updated.

    URL: http://intranet.on.ca/~sshah/booklist.html

Recommending Reading (Vehicles of the Future)

This is the recommended reading list for the Conference on Basic Research Needs for the Vehicles of the Future, sponsored in 1995 by the Princeton Materials Institute.

    URL: http://pmi.princeton.edu/conference/futurevehicles/
        appD.html

DIET, FOOD, AND NUTRITION

Alt.support.diet Bibliography and Recommended Reading List

This bibliography is part of the FAQ for the USENET newsgroup, alt.support.diet. It includes books and articles on diets, eating disorders and nutrition.

URL: http://www.ionet.net/~kchurch/biblio.html

Very Lowfat Cookbooks

This is a list of cookbooks in which at least two-thirds of the recipes have 15 percent percent of less of their fat from calories.

URL: http://www.fatfree.com/FAQ/non-vegetarian-
cookbooks

ECOLOGY AND NATURAL HISTORY

Recommended Dinosaur Reading

This is an annotated booklist of recommended dinosaur books for the general reader, selected by Phill Vanderschaegen.

URL: http://desargues.ucsd.edu/projects95/
Dinosaur.References/DINOS.HTM#reading

Sustainable Development:An Annotated Bibliography of Literature Since 1990

This bibliography is the result of an extensive literature search and review by the members of a graduate level course in Sustainable Development at the University of New York, College of Environmental Science and Forestry, Syracuse. Each work includes a review and controlled keywords designating the time scale, geographic scope, environmental focus and topical orientation of the work. The work was edited by Ralph A. Sanders and is presented as part of the Earth Pledge Home Page, which includes "Otherwise," a bimonthly book review on sustainable development and the ecosystems affected by development.

URL: http://earthpledge.org/otherwise/v1n2/annotbib.html

EDUCATION

Bibliography of Financial Aid Resource Materials

This list by Mark Kantrowitz, is part of the FinAid Home Page. It's a comprehensive listing of over 300 books on financial aid. The list has indexes for various special topics, such as type of aid, source of aid, special populations (minorities, disabled students, veterans, etc.), study abroad, and other sources of money, such as entrepreneurship. Because the list is so complete, a handy feature is a separate, much shorter list of highly recommended titles. This should be a great resource for both public and academic libraries.

URL: http://www.cs.cmu.edu/afs/cs.cmu.edu/user/mkant/
Public/FinAid/ann_bib/ann_bib.html

Home Schooling Bibliography

Karl M. Bunday maintains this extensive list of home schooling books from his own experience as well as the recommendations of participants in the online home schooling conferences on Prodigy, CompuServe, and America Online.

gopher: //lib.NMSU.EDU:70/00/.subjects/Education/
Homeschooling/Homeschooling%20Bibliography

Recommended Reading for Teachers

This eclectic and idiosyncratic list was created by Dr. Ron Pendleton of the Adult/Vocational Teacher Education Program at California State University, San Bernadino. These are not books about education, per se, but good reading to develop the minds and souls of teachers.

URL: http://www.wp.com/DRPENDLETON/books.html

Literacy Bibliography

This is an interesting literacy booklist from the Austin (Texas) Public Library.

URL: http://www.ci.austin.tx.us/LB/LBLBBIBL.HTM

HEALTH AND MEDICINE

Natural Health, Natural Healing: a Selected Bibliography (Boston Public Library)

This is a good, basic annotated booklist on natural and alternative health care from the Boston Public Library.

URL: gopher://bpl.org/00gopher_root%3a%
5bbpl_info.book_lists%5dnatural_health.doc

Ebola Recommended Reading List

This reading list is by Stephan Spencer of the Institute for Molecular Virology, and includes books, articles, references to television programs, and a link back to the University of Wisconsin's Virology Home Page.

URL: http://www.bocklabs.wisc.edu/ebola.html

INCIID Recommended Reading List (International Council on Infertility Information)

This is an annotated list of recent, recommended books for couples seeking treatment for fertility problems.

URL: http://www.mnsinc.com/inciid/bookl.html

Home Birth Literature Review

This is an extensive bibliography on home birth, with most references being to articles in American, Canadian, and British medical and nursing journals. This bibliography is the work of Ina May Gaskin, of The Farm Midwives.

URL: http://www.gaia.org/farm/lifestyle/midsearch.html

Alzheimer's Association Reading Lists

The Benjamin B. Greenfield Library of the Alzheimer's Association offers a series of well-organized, annotated booklists on various aspects of Alzheimer's Disease. In addition to "Alzheimer's Disease: a Selected List for the General Public," there are many specialized lists for both professionals and family members, including "Information for Children and Adolescents" and "Activities for Alzheimer's Patients."

http://www.alz.org/lib/rlists/Top.html

HISTORY

Reading List and Other Resources (George Washington)

The Mount Vernon Home Page includes biographical information about George Washington, and two reading lists, one for students and one for teachers.

URL: http://www.mountvernon.org/image/bioreading.html

U.S. Civil War Reading List

This is the official reading list for the USENET newsgroup alt.war.civil.usa, designed to provide the beginning Civil War reader with a short guide to introductory books. It is divided into sections, including General Histories of the War, Causes of the War, History to 1861, Slavery and Southern Society, etc., each with between three and eight books. The list is well-annotated and provides a good general overview of Civil War literature. It is maintained by Stephen Schmidt.

URL: http://www.cis.ohio-state.edu/hypertext/faq/usenet-faqs/bygroup/soc/history/_civil-war-usa%3areading-list.html

Civil War Reading List

This list, compiled by Mark Pitcavage, is an alternative to the list above. This list is also divided into sections, including Army Histories, Strategy, and Diplomacy. This list includes more titles than the previous list, including titles included for historiographical significance.

> URL: http://www.greyware.com/authors/pitman/
> civilwar.htm

Bibliography: Religion in Sixteenth and Seventeenth Century England

This is a bibliography by Charles Nethaway on the religious background of the English settlers who came to the American colonies in the seventeenth century.

> URL: http://www.clark.net/pub/cnethawa/relig003.html

Richard III Society Reading Lists

"Ricardian Reading" is a well-organized, annotated bibliography, offering works written at a variety of levels for students of history as well as professional historians. The first section, "A Ricardian Primer," includes biographies, background histories, and fiction, and there are also separate listings on various topics, including "The Murder of the Princes," "The Pretenders," and "The Battle of Bosworth." The last section is a list of published and online bibliographies.

> URL: http://www.webcom.com/~blanchrd/biblio.html

LITERATURE

Science Fiction and Fantasy Author Bibliographies

These author bibliographies of current and classic Science Fiction and Fantasy authors are almost entirely the work of one man, the indefatigable John Wenn, who posted them individually to the SF-Lovers e-mail group. These lists are great for helping readers find out which books belong to which series, and in what order.

> URL: http://julmara.ce.chalmers.se:80/SF_archive/
> Authorlists/

Vampire Fiction

This reading list of vampire fiction is associated with the USENET newsgroup alt.vampyres, and includes books suggested and reviewed by members of that group. The list is maintained by David C. Mudie.

> URL: http://radon.eecs.berkeley.edu/~mudie/vampfic.html

Usenet Alternate History List

The USENET Alternate History List is an annotated list of fiction involving altered history, for example, stories about what might have happened if the South had won the Civil War or the Nazis had won World War II. The list is maintained by R.B. Schmunk and is posted regularly to rec.arts.sf.written and alt.history.what-if.

URL: http://anansi.panix.com/userdirs/rbs/AH/

Literature and Languages: Selected Reading Lists (Chicago Public Library)

The Literature and Languages Division of the Harold Washington Library Center have the text of many of their reading lists on the Chicago Public Library Home Page. Lists include "Fiction and Poetry by Native Americans," "Horrors! Selected Supernatural Fiction," "Exploring the Possibilities: Coming of Age Novels in the Fiction Collection," "Star Trek: Selected Fiction," and "Gay and Lesbian Drama Reading List." There are also a few lists with a Chicago slant, including "Murder in Chicago: A Selected List of Mystery Fiction with a Chicago setting."

URL: http://cpl.lib.uic.edu/001hwlc/litlists/litlists.html

Books for Adults (Boston Public Library)

The Boston Public Library has a number of interesting booklists, including "East Meets West: Fiction by Chinese American and Chinese British Writers," "From Book Store to Box Office: Famous Books on the Silver Screen," and "Knockout Sports Novels."

URL: gopher://bpl.org/11gopher_root%3a%5bbpl_
info.book_lists.adults%5d

Horror: 100 Best Books

A chronological listing of the best 100 horror books, selected by polling horror authors for their favorites. This list is part of "The Cabinet of Dr. Casey," Casey Hopkins's Horror Web Site, which also includes author bibliographies, and other useful resources.

URL: http://www.cat.pdx.edu/~caseyh/horror/top100.html

Recommended Science Fiction and Fantasy

This is an extensive list of Science Fiction and Fantasy recommended by the members of the USENET newsgroup rec.arts.sf/written.robert-jordan. The list is divided into categories including Highly Recommended, Mixed Recommendations, Fewer Recommendations, etc., depending on the responses of the group.

Most entries have brief, informal recommendations. The list is maintained by Andrea Leistra.

> URL: http://www-leland.stanford.edu/~aleistra/booklist.html

The NESFA Reading List of Core SF and Fantasy

This list is compiled by Mark L. Olson for the New England Science Fiction Association. It includes novels, short stories, and important relevant nonfiction. There are no annotations, but there are codes designating why the work may be considered core, recommendation in standard works, for example.

> URL: http://worcester.lm.com/nesfa/nesfacor.html

Children's Literature Home Page

This World Wide Web site, created by David K. Brown of the University of Calgary, is the best single site for all types of information related to Children's Literature. It includes links to all the author home pages, awards, and recommended reading lists, e-mail and USENET newsgroups, and other academic sites related to Children's Literature.

> URL: http://www.ucalgary.ca/~dkbrown/index.html

PHILOSOPHY, PSYCHOLOGY, AND RELIGION

Contemporary Philosophy of Mind: An Annotated Bibliography

This is an excellent, authoritative resource, with over 1800 citations to books and journal articles on the philosophy of mind, the philosophy of cognitive science, and the philosophy of artificial intelligence. The booklist is well-organized and most entries are annotated. This project is the work of David Chalmers of the Department of Philosophy, Washington University, St. Louis.

> URL: http://www.artsci.wustl.edu/~chalmers/biblio.html

Self-Help Center

This is an interesting project from the University of Missouri that could be helpful for collection development. The Self-Help Center is an online list of recommended self-help books. The first page is the index, listing topics such as Family, Career Development, Death and Dying, Abuse, and Eating Disorders. Selecting one of those links brings you to a list of recommended titles, and selecting a title gets you full bibliographic information plus a summary.

> URL: http://www.missouri.edu/~councwww/self_help/index.html

Recommended Readings

This is another listing of self-help books from the Counseling Center of the University of New York at Buffalo. Subjects include Stress Management, Meditation, and Inner Healing.

   http://wings.buffalo.edu/student-life/ccenter/Readings/

Recommended Reading and Listening for Wild Women

This is a reading list compiled for the Wild Wolf Women of the Web, an e-mail group for the exploration of the wild woman archetype. Readers of the 1992 bestseller, "Women Who Run with the Wolves," by Clarissa Pinkola Estes, will find some interesting reading suggestions. The list also includes books on tape and some suggested musical listening.

   URL: http://www.lisp.com/~annie/resource.html

Coming Out Reading List

This list is from the Gay, Lesbian, and Bisexual student organization at Indiana University. It is divided into two parts: books that deal directly with the issue of coming out, and books that have been suggested as providing helpful background information or inspiration.

   URL: http://www.indiana.edu/~iu_glb/
          comingout.reading.list.html

Depression Book List

This list by Dan Ash is posted regularly to the USENET newsgroup alt.support.depression.

   URL: http://www.cis.ohio-state.edu/hypertext/faq/usenet/
          alt-support-depression/books.etx/faq.html

Books on OCD (Obsessive Compulsive Disorder) and Related Disorders

This is a useful list, although like many Internet lists, it is still developing and could benefit from more complete citations.

   URL: http://www.fairlite.com/ocd/books/

Anxiety Booklist

Noodles Panic-Anxiety Page has a section for reviews of books on anxiety, panic disorders, and related conditions. Each book has one or more reviews or personal recommendations from visitors to the site. This is an informal personal exchange of information about helpful books.

   URL: http://frank.mtsu.edu/~sward/anxiety/books.html

Post-Traumatic Stress Disorder Bibliography

This is an annotated bibliography from Veritas Publishing on Post-Traumatic Stress Syndrome as it relates to survivors of war, sexual abuse, physical abuse, crime, and other severe trauma.

    URL: http://www.sover.net/~schwcof/ptsd.html

Annotated Science/Faith Bibliography

This excellent bibliography is by Keith B. Miller of the Department of Geology of the Kansas State University. It has sections on the integration of science and scripture, theology of creation, and Christian environmentalism.

    URL: http://www.ksu.edu/~kbmill/scifaith.html

Quaker Bibliography

This annotated bibliography by Joel Gazis-Sax is part of the soc.religion.quaker FAQ.

    URL: http://www.quaker.org/book-list.html

Judaism Reading Lists

The Judaism Reading Lists are compiled and maintained by Daniel J. Faigin to support the discussion on soc.culture.jewish, and they have become one of the best-organized booklist projects on the Internet. There are several different reading lists on different aspects of Judaism and Jewish life, and each list is further divided into more specific subject areas. The titles are carefully selected and annotated.

This is also a model project in terms of distribution. The lists are posted regularly to soc.culture.jewish, soc.answers, and news.answers. They are also available at NYSERNETs Shamash, a web server devoted to Judaism. Using the Web versions is especially convenient, allowing easy access to each lists subtopics, which are nicely divided and labelled.

    URL: http://shamash.nysernet.org/

Ethiopian Jewry: NACOEJ Selected Reading List

The North American Conference on Ethiopian Jewry maintains an excellent list of books and articles about Ethiopian Jews, with some recommended background reading on Ethiopia in general. It includes separate sections listing reading for children and young adults.

    URL: http://www.cais.com/nacoej/18.html

Baha'i Faith Annotated Bibliography

This is an annotated bibliography of works about the teachings of Baha'u'llah and the Baha'i Faith.

URL: http://www.bcca.org/services/srb/biblio.html

Mythology

This site includes the following series of mythology bibiographies: Asatru Bibliography, Astromythology Bibliography, British Bibliography, Camelot: History Bibliography (Arthur's Britain), Celtic Bibliography, Celtic Reading List, Druid Bibliography, Feudal Bibliography, Mycenaean Mysteries Bibliography, Norse Mythology Bibliography, Old Irish Bibliography, Seidhr Bibliography, Shamanism Bibliography and Sumerian Bibliography.

URL: http://www.the-wire.com/culture/mythology/
mythbibl.html

SOCIAL ISSUES

What Are Some Good Men's Movement Books?

The Men's Issues Page includes a lengthy list of books related to the Men's Movement, with notes from a team of reviewers. Most of the titles are recent but selected older titles are included for a historical perspective.

This booklist has an informal, almost interactive, feel with personal recommendations and comments from the reviewers, and many hypertext links to additional reviews.

URL: http://www.vix.com/pub/men/books/reviews.html

Core Lists in Womens Studies

The Collection Development and Bibliography Committee of the Women's Studies Section, Association of College and Research Libraries, has developed a series of Core Lists in Womens Studies, designed for collection development in Womens Studies and to assist faculty members in selecting course readings.

Each list includes twenty to fifty titles that are currently listed in *Books in Print,* with the most important five to ten titles starred. The lists are updated every January, dropping titles that are no longer in print and adding important new works. The individual lists cover various aspects of womens studies, including "Women of Color in the United States," "History of Women in the United States," and "Sexual Abuse." Although the lists are intended to support academic libraries, they would also be helpful for public librarians doing collection development, readers' advisory work, book displays, and more.

This is a well-defined and well-organized project that uses the

Internet for resource sharing; in this case, to share the efforts and expertise of a dedicated group of librarians.

The Core Lists are distributed by the office of the University of Wisconsin System Women' Studies Librarian.

URL: http://www.library.wisc.edu/libraries/
WomensStudies/#corelists

Wisconsin Bibliographies in Women's Studies

Another valuable project available from the office of the University of Wisconsin Women's Studies Librarian is the collection of Wisconsin Bibliographies in Women's Studies, including many that would be useful for any public or academic library. A few examples include "Issues Related to Women in Management," "Ecofeminism: an Introductory Bibliography," and "Women Mystery Writers."

URL: http://www.library.wisc.edu/libraries/
WomensStudies/#bibliographies

Prison Awareness Project Reading List

This is a concise, annotated list of books about prisons and crime.

URL: http://www.halcyon.com/dante/pap/reading.html

Recommended Reading: Assault Prevention Information Network

This is an annotated list of books on self-defense and personal safety, including firearms.

URL: http://www.en.utexas.edu/studentprojects/syverson/
apin/BookList.html

SPORTS, HOBBIES AND RECREATION

Ballooning Books and Periodicals

This list, by Eric E. Goodson, is part of the Ballooning Online home page. It includes adult and children's fiction, nonfiction, reference works, and periodicals.

URL: http://sunsite.unc.edu/ballooning/balloon-
media.html

Reading Suggestions (Bullfighting)

This is a list of fiction and nonfiction related to bullfighting, maintained by Javier Bustamante as part of the Hispanic Heritage Home Page.

http://www.clark.net/pub/jgbustam/toros/bullbook.html

TRAVEL AND REGIONAL STUDIES

Irish Books for the holidays

This article by Martin Russell, Poetry/Book Editor of the Irish American Post, was written as a guide for Christmas shoppers in 1994, but it's a well-selected and well-described list of interesting books about Ireland and the Irish that would be helpful for book talks, book displays, reading groups, etc.

    URL: http://celtic.stanford.edu/pub/post/Dec/Books

Books of Cajun interest

This booklist, part of Chuck Taggart's GumboWeb, is an interesting selection of books on the people of Acadiana and their culture, with a special emphasis on music.

    URL: http://www.webcom.com/~gumbo/acadiana/cajun-books.html

Welcome to America Reading List

This booklist is available from a Dutch Web site, and is intended for Europeans who plan to visit or just want to understand the United States. The list includes ten titles, mostly recent, on American political and social issues. This is a thought-provoking list that could be interesting for a book talk or reading group.

    URL: http://huizen.dds.nl/~seismo/readusa.html

Balkan Booklist

This is an annotated booklist from Bosnia Briefings that provides recent works on the effects of the war in Bosnia as well as works that provide a historical background on the Balkan region.

    URL: http://www.ikon.com/bosnia/briefings/books.html

Moon Travel Handbooks: Asia and South Pacific Travel Booklists

Moon makes the booklists from their travel books available at the Web site. Each annotated list includes works about the language, history, and culture of the people, making these lists a good starting point for the student as well as the traveller. Currently available are lists for Japan, South Korea, Nepal, Thailand, Indonesia, Australia, New Zealand, and the South Pacific.

    URL: http://www.moon.com:80/bklist/bkfront.html

Lonely Planet

Lonely Planet also offers the booklists from their travel books.

Follow the link to each destination, for a listing of available information, including the Recommended Reading list.

 URL: http://www.lonelyplanet.com/dest/dest.htm

Selected Bibliography: Irish Nationalism, Republicanism, and General History

This booklist by Jacqueline Dana is part of the Irish Political Prisoner Information site.

 URL: http://wwwvms.utexas.edu/~jdana/biblio.html

UFOs, ASTROLOGY, AND PARANORMAL PHENOMENA

UFO Books—The Serious Literature

This is an extensive, annotated bibliography by Keith Rowell of the works by serious UFO researchers, those who fall between what Rowell calls "the naive believers and the fanatic debunkers."

 URL: http://www.cs.bgsu.edu/~jzawodn/ufo/ufo-
   books.html

Skeptic Annotated Bibliography

This is a lengthy, highly organized bibliography of books on paranormal and fringe science topics, from a skeptical point of view. Topics include UFOs, astrology, the Bermuda Triangle, ancient astronauts, crop circles, parapsychology, etc.

 http://www.public.iastate.edu/~edis/skeptic_biblio.html

Astrology: Recommended Reading

This is a list of recommended astrology books, from Astrology Plus.

 URL: http://www.smart.net/~astro/books.html

INDEX

COLOPHON

Elizabeth B. Thomsen held positions as Children's Librarian, Young Adult Services Librarian, and Technical Services Librarian in the public libraries of Salem, Hamilton, Revere, and Wakefield, Massachusetts. She is currently the Member Services Manager of NOBLE, the North of Boston Library Exchange, a consortium of twenty-four public and academic libraries. She is also a partner in Library Management Associates, with experience in library building programs, technology planning, training, and meeting facilitation, and the listowner of several literary e-mail groups.

Other Titles of Interest in the *Neal-Schuman NetGuide* Series

FINDING GOVERNMENT INFORMATION ON THE INTERNET:
A How-To-Do-It Manual
Edited by John Maxymuk

"For librarians and anyone else with interest in government information policy, this book offers the most comprehensive overview available of government information on the Internet . . . thorough and well-documented . . ." *Library Journal*

1-55570-228-7. 1995. 8 1/2 x 11.
175 pp. $39.95.

THE INTERNET SEARCHER'S HANDBOOK
Locating Information, People, and Software

Novice or advanced Internet searchers can use this handy resource to conduct comprehensive research investigations—and find the answers to quick reference queries. The book provides in-depth coverage on virtual libraries, Internet directories, communities of people, and Internet search tools, plus examples of real searches for each resource.

1-55570-243-0. 1996. 8 1/2 x 11.
240 pp. $35.00.

USING THE WORLD WIDE WEB AND CREATING HOME PAGES:
A How-To-Do-It Manual for Librarians
by Ray E. Metz and Gail Junion-Metz

The first and only manual specifically designed to help you browse the Web, *Using the World Wide Web and Creating Home Pages* demonstrates how to integrate the Web into your library services, and build a home page for your library that will be the toast of the electronic community.

1-55570-241-4. 1996. 8 1/2 x 11.
200 pp. $45.00.

THE COMPLETE INTERNET COMPANION FOR LIBRARIANS
by Allen C. Benson

"An effective road map for new drivers on the information superhighway, teaching not only the rules of the road but also showing how to deal with roadblocks and detours." *Library Journal*

1-55570-178-7. 1995. 8 1/2 x 11.
405 pp. $49.95.

LEARNING THE INTERNET:
A Workbook for Beginners
by John Burke

Learn the Internet interactively with this field-tested, hands-on workbook that guides you through all of the Internet basics with creative and detailed activities that will teach you and re-inforce your skills—and are fun to do! Using it is like attending a workshop on using the Net, one that will allow you to work at your own pace and at times convenient to you.

1-55570-248-1. 1996. 8 1/2 x 11.
150 pp. $29.95.

THE INTERNET ACCESS COOKBOOK:
A Librarian's Commonsense Guide to Low-Cost Connections
by Karen G. Schneider

"What distinguishes this title from the glut of Internet books in print is its ability to empower a computer novice with the knowledge and confidence to successfully plan and connect to the Internet. Schneider, *American Libraries*' 'Internet Librarian' columnist . . . covers everything. This is recommended. Bon appetit!" *Library Journal*

1-55570-235-X. 1995. 6 x 9.
322 pp. $24.95.

THE INTERNET COMPENDIUM: GUIDES TO RESOURCES BY SUBJECT
By Louis Rosenfeld, Joseph Janes, and Martha Vander Kolk

A unique series compiled by a team from the acclaimed University of Michigan Internet Clearinghouse that provides direct location access to a virtual mall of over ten thousand Internet addresses in hundreds of subjects.

Subject Guides to Humanities Resources
1-55570-218-X. 1995.
8 1/2 x 11. 368 pp. $75.00.

Subject Guides to Health and Science Resources
1-55570-219-8. 1995.
8 1/2 x 11. 529 pp. $75.00.

Subject Guides to Social Sciences, Business & Law
1-55570-220-1. 1995.
8 1/2 x 11. 424 pp. $75.00.

Buy all three subject guides for $175
1-55570-188-4.

" . . . a good choice for anyone who wants to avoid the distractions other books offer." *College & Research Libraries News*

USING THE INTERNET, ONLINE SERVICES, AND CD-ROMs FOR WRITING RESEARCH AND TERM PAPERS
Edited by Charles Harmon

This unique guide is a basic, comprehensive manual for high school and college students that does for electronic resources what Turabian does for print. Includes MLA and APA citation formats for Internet and CD-ROM sources.

1-55570-238-4. 1996. 6 x 9.
150 pp. $29.95.

Publication dates, prices, and number of pages for new titles may be estimates and are subject to change.

To order or request further information, contact:
Neal-Schuman Publishers
100 Varick Street, New York, NY 10013
212-925-8650
or fax toll free—1-800-584-2414